ERICA ROSE

MAGICAL EVER AFTER

Manifesting Your Fairy-Tale Romance with Angels, Mermaids and Faeries

Foreword by Karen Kay

Published by Muse Oracle Press Pty Ltd

Title: *Magical Ever After: Manifesting Your Fairy-Tale Romance with Angels, Mermaids & Faeries*
Author: Erica Rose
Editing by: Kim Fairminer

ISBN: 978-1-7635869-4-9
First published in 2025 by Muse Oracle Press Pty Ltd
Distributed by Red Wheel Weiser Books
museoraclepress.com

Printed in China

This publication is intended for informational and inspirational purposes only. It reflects the personal experiences, opinions, and spiritual beliefs of the author. It is not intended as a substitute for professional medical, psychological, legal, or financial advice. The practices and suggestions in this book are offered in good faith but come with no guarantee of results. Individual outcomes will vary based on numerous factors. The author and publisher disclaim all liability in connection with the use of this material.

References to third-party trademarks, television shows, or musical works are the property of their respective owners and are used in this book for editorial and illustrative purposes only. No sponsorship, endorsement, or affiliation is implied.

Dedication: *To my angel watching me from the other side, my mother Alice. Thank you for having welcomed me into this world with true love.*

Foreword

By Karen Kay, Fairy Whisperer
for *Magical Ever After – Manifesting Your Fairy-Tale Romance with Angels, Mermaids, and Faeries*
by Erica Rose

Once upon a time, in an enchanted garden, an open-hearted little girl listened closely—and she heard the whispers of the fairies. Among the roses, the fae softly called to her, and she never stopped listening.
That little girl was me.

Since that magical beginning in my grandmother's garden, the fairies have never left my side, guiding me through joyful and challenging moments, nudging me gently toward joy, healing, magic, and love. Their presence is not something I imagined—it's something I live. Fairies are not fantasy. They are real and an integral part of our beautiful, breathing planet. They are the guardians of nature.

When I first heard about *Magical Ever After*, I felt the 'fairy fizzes'! It's like the tingles or goosebumps, but with a fairy twist! Erica Rose has written a magical love letter, a shimmering guide that will not only help to restore your faith and belief in love, but also help you manifest it through the divine guidance of fairies, mermaids, angels, and magical beings.

Before we dive into the book, let's take a moment to remember what love felt like before the world and personal circumstances implied it was difficult to find.

When we were children, we wholeheartedly believed in happily-ever-afters. We believed a kiss could break a curse, that someone out there was meant just for us, and that magical beings watched over every step we took. We believed in signs from the divine, in fairy godmothers, and in songs that made flowers bloom and woodland animals run to us.

But somewhere along the way, the challenges of adult life took over, and we started to see love portrayed not as something magical, but messy. We sang along to heartbreaking ballads, watched stories of betrayal unfold on screen, and were told again and again that our standards were too high. We learned to almost expect disappointment. And some of us forgot the enchantment of longing, the divine timing of soul connections, and the sacred energy that flows between kindred spirits.

But what if that story—the one that says love is hard to find—isn't true?

What if your fairy-tale romance was never just a dream, but a premonition of a wonderful future reality? Your very own *Magical Ever After*?

Well, that's exactly what Erica reminds us of in this delightful and enchanting book. She invites you to remember and return to the truth you knew as a child: that love is real, love is magical, and love is absolutely yours to manifest. With a magical wave of her metaphorical wand of words, she rekindles hope and joy.

As someone who has spent her life whispering with fairies, I can tell you with complete heartfelt certainty that everything that grows has a fairy guardian. Every blossom, every blade of grass, every fruit on the vine is lovingly watched over by a magical spirit of nature. These fae beings are not figments of your imagination—they are as real as real can be. They are the keepers of the Earth's energy and the original caretakers of our precious planet.

That's why I created my *Oracle of the Fairies*—to help others tune into their guidance. And it's why I was so delighted to see Erica channelling these spirits of nature to help people manifest their soul-aligned romantic partners. In this book, you'll learn how to open your energy field to love by working with angels, fairies, and the mermaids. What's not to love?

I was so excited to see Erica include these oceanic mer-beings of intuition and sensuality. In my own deck, *Messages from the Mermaids*, I've shared how they help us dive into the depths of our emotions, clearing away fear and illusion so we can rise to the surface with clarity and confidence, and take a deep dive into our hearts to open to love again, if we wish—even if that love affair is a rekindling of self-love or with a partner.

I adore the way Erica invites you into a relationship with these beings. She doesn't treat them like characters in a storybook, but as the sacred, sentient guides they truly are. She also offers beautiful meditations to help you introduce yourself to your fairy and mermaid allies, opening portals of connection that, with continued practice, can deepen over time.

What makes *Magical Ever After* extra powerful is its deep-rooted understanding that manifestation isn't just about "thinking positively." It's about aligning your energetic frequency with the love you desire. That means healing your heart, raising your vibration, and becoming a magnetic match for your most romantic dreams.

Erica's personal story is a shining example of this. Like many of us, she'd experienced heartbreak, disappointment, and the sting of feeling overlooked. But instead of dimming her light, she turned inward. She remembered her power. She began working intentionally with the same magical beings that had helped her in other areas of life. And once she aligned her energy, the Universe responded. And now she is truly shining her light in this book to share with all.

What happened next reads like a rom-com directed by the fae: serendipitous meetings, synchronicities, and a friendship that blossomed into a deep, soul-satisfying romance—complete with snowflakes at Bryant Park, a kiss in the rain during *Hamlet*, and finally, a proposal in front of the Eiffel Tower—fairy-tale perfection, grounded in very real magic. Proving that dreams and wishes really can and do come true!

If Erica can manifest her *Magical Ever After*, then so can you!

Fairy magic isn't about escaping reality—far from it! It's about enhancing it. It's about recognizing that love is not just a feeling, but a frequency. And when you work with the elements—Earth, Air, Fire, Water (and Spirit)—you can activate the divine love codes already residing within you.

This book is full of practical and magical tools to help you do just that.

You'll find rituals, affirmations, meditations, visualizations, and more. You'll learn how to co-create with the Universe, how to heal past heartbreaks, and how to craft a love story that mirrors your most authentic self.

As Erica wisely reminds us, we must never attempt to manifest a specific person—that would override their free will, and this is something I strongly agree with. Instead, this book will help you call in your perfect energetic match: someone who is aligned with your highest good, someone whose soul recognizes yours as home. All it takes is faith, trust, and a sprinkle of pixie dust!

Whether you're just starting your manifestation journey or are a seasoned spiritual practitioner, this book has something to offer wherever you are on your path. And it does so with the most important ingredient of all: joy.

That's the essence of fairy magic—joy, beauty, play, and a reverence for life's mysteries.

So, light a candle, play soft music, gather your crystals, turn on your fairy lights, and let this book be your companion. Let it awaken your heart, soothe your spirit, and remind you that you were never too much, and you are enough, exactly as you are.

It's time, dear friend.
Time to let the fairies guide you.
Time to listen to the mermaids sing.
Time to trust the whispers of Spirit.
Time to manifest your magical ever after.

Because you deserve it. You always have.
And now… you're ready.

With love, light, joy, and magical fairy blessings,

Karen Kay
The Fairy Whisperer
www.karenkay.co.uk
Author of *Fairy Whispering: 111 Magical Practices for Connecting with the Fairies*, *Messages from the Mermaids*, *Oracle of the Fairies*, and *Manifesting with the Fairies*

Foreword To Magical Ever After

By Kim Fairminer, Astrologer, Author, Editor
for *Magical Ever After – Manifesting Your Fairy-Tale Romance with Angels, Mermaids, and Faeries*
by Erica Rose

Like you, dear reader, my quest to find love had many twists and turns. For a time, I feared I might be lost forever in the dark forest. And while retreating from the world to live quietly in a cute cottage on the edge of the forest holds a certain appeal, picking up this book tells me you aren't quite ready to jump into that reality.

My devious wolves were fleeting encounters that fizzled as quickly as they'd sparked. And although it felt like it at the time, I wasn't cursed when my first marriage imploded after 18 months. (I jokingly refer to it as my "Hollywood marriage" because it was so short!) Returning to single life in my 30s felt as overwhelming as spinning straw into gold overnight. I even took up jogging at one point, hoping to outrun my frustrations. Drastic, I know.

Finding true love is a journey — unpredictable, riveting, a wild ride all of its own. Thankfully, Erica has a way of sprinkling whimsy and magic on an aspect of life that so many of us feel fraught and awkward about.

When matters of the heart aren't working out as we hope, we feel vulnerable, disconnected, and forsaken. And when we find ourselves in this emotionally undone state, it can be tempting to either avoid the issue or turn to logic as the solution. The modern world champions intellectual analysis, so why not track your dating stats on a spreadsheet and ask an AI bot how to meet your perfect match?

Why not? Because love isn't logical; it's magical!

Love is the most powerful force in the universe. It inspires art, ignites passion, and moves us in ways mysterious and profound. More logic won't welcome love into your life. The world needs more empathy, more connection, and more awareness of soul. For love to flow freely and abundantly, we need to welcome magic into our lives.

And this book tells you how. In *Magical Ever After*, Erica flings open the castle gates, rolls out the red carpet, and ushers you into a new way of seeing and experiencing the world—with the specific goal of meeting your true love.

Erica's life experience has led her to ask: What if love isn't just a matter of luck or chance? What if it was possible to manifest love tangibly in our lives — not through manipulation, but through the magic of intention and energy? What if you could write your own love story?

Erica found her spiritual path early in life and found her true love by committing to living a magical life. She knows what works.

In this book, she'll guide you to reconnect with your magic. In every sentence, she embodies the magic of love (and the love of magic) and generously shares her wisdom with anyone willing to open their heart. If you follow her teachings, you will plug back into your magical connection with the Universe so that love can flow into your life, freely and abundantly.

It's important to suspend your disbelief and lean into your fairytale romance — this is central to Erica's teachings. Not only does she articulate a clear vision (clarity of intention is critical to successful spellwork), but her methodology for getting to your outcome, to your magical ever after, is metaphysically sound and easily adaptable to your personal circumstances and preferences.

In *Magical Ever After*, Erica invites you to step into the enchanting world where magic meets the law of attraction, offering a heart-centred approach to calling in the relationship you desire. This isn't a book about casting spells to control another's will — far from it. Instead, Erica guides you in aligning your energy, clarifying your desires, and becoming a magnet for the kind of love that truly nourishes your soul — a love rooted in re-enchanting your life with intention and wonder.

Globally, the longing for authentic connection and a renewed sense of wonder is deepening. Erica's work fills this gap, blending modern manifestation techniques with timeless magical practices. She weaves together rituals, affirmations, and energy work with practical advice, reminding us that magic is not about wishful thinking — it's about focused intention, self-awareness, and co-creating with the Universe.

Reading the manuscript for *Magical Ever After*, I found myself falling in love with my husband of 14 years all over again. (See? I'm another success story. As Erica often says, it absolutely will happen.) While I didn't manifest him — consciously at least — magic was an intrinsic part of that period of my life (and still is). Erica weaves intention and enchantment into her methods, an approach that resonated with me deeply and reminded me that love blooms when we open ourselves to the Universe's hidden currents.

All those years ago, my single friend and I joined an online dating site — on April Fool's Day. We chose the date intentionally and playfully. As Erica recommends, this action told the Universe that we were open to its magic. I didn't meet my husband via the dating site though. We met on my front porch through my housemate because they shared a niece. I set him up on a blind date with another friend, which didn't work out (in fact, it was a small-scale disaster), so I invited him out to commiserate. (Erica covers how unexpected chains of events can lead you to your true love.)

Being newly single in this period of my life, my priorities had shifted significantly. My expectations of setting up a house and beginning my life as a newlywed in tatters, I threw myself into my spiritual practice, worked hard, and booked trips overseas. I went to Japan with my online dating friend (when she had just found out she was pregnant to someone she'd met on the dating platform — they are still married too!) and had also booked my trip of a lifetime — an astrological tour of Egypt. (It was much later that I discovered both Japan and Egypt were on my natal Venus lines. Venus, of course, is the planet of love.)

I remember sitting on a beautifully woven carpet with a blind fortune teller in Siwa Oasis, making the biggest decision of my life. That reading posed a question that has had life-changing consequences. I chose to believe what was in my heart. I chose to believe in my happily ever after with the man who is now my husband.

The oracles, the synchronicities, the energetic shifts — I recognised all these features of my own love story in Erica's methodology. While I'm well-versed in magic and divination, you don't have to be an expert to work with the unseen support that surrounds you. You just need to believe. Erica will step you through exactly what you need to know, who you need to know (angels, mermaids, and fairies!), and what you (importantly) need to do.

Romanticising your life and embracing a fairy-tale romance isn't about chasing illusions — it's about shifting your perception to see the magic already woven through your everyday experiences. It's the art of noticing small gestures of kindness, cherishing fleeting moments of beauty, and treating your life as a wondrous, unfurling miracle. When you tend to love — whether it's through a soft glance, a thoughtful word, or simply creating space for joy — you draw more of that energy into your world.

This isn't passive dreaming; it's an intentional practice of nurturing connection and inviting enchantment into your reality. By doing so (there's that word again—doing! Love is action!), love ceases to be a distant fantasy and instead becomes a living, breathing presence in your life. Your life is the magic.

This book is more than a guide; it's a trusted companion for anyone who has ever longed for a deep, meaningful connection. Erica writes as a skilled practitioner and a passionate advocate, offering both practical instructions and enthusiastic encouragement. She wholeheartedly believes in the transformative power of love—for nurturing yourself and for attracting the relationships you desire.

I encourage you to open your heart and mind as you read these pages. Let Erica's buoyant generosity of spirit convince you that magic is real, love is abundant, and that you have the power to manifest the fulfilling partnership you seek.

May your journey through these pages be as magical as the love that awaits you.

Kim Fairminer
Astrologer, Author, Editor

Contents

Once Upon a Time...

When we were little kids, we were shown love through the lens of rose-colored glasses. We read stories about the magic of true love's kiss. We watched movies where happily ever after came after the star-crossed couple *finally* got together. We saw love as a fairy tale, a romantic dream come true, and everything anyone could ever want in a lifetime.

Then, we grew up, and our rose-colored glasses cracked. We watched movies that glorified dramatic romances. We heard stories of once-happy couples fighting through nasty divorces. We experienced people in relationships who lied, cheated, and broke their promises. We belted out songs about being heartbroken; *we had our hearts broken*. We were convinced by society that love doesn't always last; we can't trust anyone; and dating, quite frankly, is the absolute worst.

These widely accepted narratives fuel the cycle of people *genuinely* believing that finding and keeping love is difficult.

The real truth is—those narratives are a lie.

The stories you believed as a child about love being a magical happily-ever-after can be your real truth.

I always held high expectations of having a fairy-tale romance, but throughout my teens and early 20s, my love life proved to be more like a Grimm's fairy tale than a Disney one.

Of all the areas of my life, love had been my biggest struggle. It was hard to see others find love so effortlessly, while it was just disappointment after disappointment for me. I was tired of repeated relationships not working out and being told my standards were too high. It was also heartbreaking to know that I just wasn't the one potential partners wanted.

After one particularly frustrating dating experience, I had my enough-is-enough moment and remembered my power in creating my reality. I knew about manifestation. I worked with spirits, like angels, faeries, and mermaids, to help me in almost every other aspect of my life, so why couldn't I work with them to manifest the love I had been dreaming of? I knew I had the power within to stop the struggle and start living the real fairy tale.

I got serious and dedicated myself to doing the inner work. I analyzed the energy of those around me who had love versus the ones who didn't. I dove into healing my romantic past, shifting my mindset around love, and working with Spirit to receive divine wisdom on how to call in everything I wanted and more.

Not long after I started making this shift, I manifested a new corporate job for a company I had once dreamed of working for. Within the first couple of months of being there, I began to click with one of my co-workers. We quickly became best friends. I couldn't help but compare how similar we were to Jim and Pam from the US version of *The Office* (an iconic couple in my eyes). The two of us were always talking and laughing about the silliest things, but we also shared deep, life conversations. We had an effortless chemistry, and while at first, neither of us had any intention other than genuine friendship, eventually, over time, we started to fall in love with each other. Since we were just friends, we both had that awkward inner monologue running through our heads: *Do they feel the same way about me? Do I tell them how I feel and risk ruining the friendship?* Neither of us wanted to ruin what we had or admit our feelings, so we kept them buried.

One December evening, things started to change.

I attended a friend's Christmas party where, at the end of the night, one of her co-workers asked me to go out on a date the following week. I reluctantly decided to go. After all, I was technically single and under the assumption my best friend would never have feelings for me.

As the date approached, I knew something felt off and wrong. I told my best friend about it, but despite what he *really* wanted to say, he encouraged me to go and have a good time as any best friend would.

On the date, as we were ice skating at Bryant Park with all the twinkling holiday lights surrounding us, snow started to float gently down from the sky, and at that moment, it hit me. I realized I didn't want to be here with this guy or anyone else. I was in love with my best friend! I wanted to be here with *him*, holding *his* hand, and being romantic on a date.

I always told the Universe I wanted a 'rom-com-esque' love story and it delivered. At the exact moment of my realization, my best friend was at the airport. I later learned that he was anxiously pacing back and forth in the terminal, distressed about me being on a date with someone else because he was finally ready to admit to himself that he was in love with me, too.

It still took a few months for things to align after that, but that summer, we *finally* went out on a real date to see a live performance of *Hamlet* in a beautiful outdoor courtyard. The play, however, was cut short due to unexpected rain, which allowed us to privately have the most magical, movie-like kiss in the rain. Finally, we fell out of the friend zone and into our romantic relationship.

Four and a half years later, my best friend proposed to me in Trocadéro across from the Eiffel Tower in Paris, a romantic nod to the Valentine's Day card he had given me every single year. We were married in a fairy-tale wedding at the Grand Floridian Resort and Spa in Walt Disney World on the sixth anniversary of that first magical kiss in the rain. Our ceremony had views of Cinderella's Castle and we even got to ride in a pumpkin-shaped carriage!

Fairy-tale romances do exist. Let my story be proof of that. I know it's no coincidence once I decided to work with my inner magic that my love life changed. I was able to manifest a divinely aligned true love and a cinematic love story that exceeded all my high expectations. I did it all by shifting my energy.

Everything is made up of energy. Our thoughts, our feelings, our bodies, our minds—every single thing in the Universe has an energetic frequency. We exist in one giant energy field, and as we learned from science class, the energy an object vibrates at and projects into the field is the same energy that will reverberate back.

Therefore, the energy *you* project is the energy that will return to you. Your thoughts and internal beliefs determine your energetic frequency. Whatever you believe to be true about the world is exactly what will come back to you and show up for you as your reality.

Your brain always wants to prove you right. It never wants you to think you're wrong. If you have genuinely accepted the narrative that love is a struggle, your brain will alert you to examples that support those internal beliefs, in your life and others' lives. Actively noticing these examples only further solidifies your story that love is arduous. This will cause you to keep projecting that energy and, in turn, receive more situations of love being difficult. It's a vicious cycle—but it doesn't have to be!

If you can recognize that your negative beliefs about love originate from outside influences—whether from bitter family members, unhappy friends, or society as a whole—it proves that these beliefs were learned, not inherent. If you learned them, you can *unlearn* them. It's possible to fill your brain with *new* beliefs that support the story of true love you want to be experiencing.

When it comes to manifesting love, your mind is your most powerful tool.

Your other most powerful tool is connecting with Spirit. Intuition isn't a rare blessing bestowed only to a lucky few; it's an innate sense that exists within all of us. Intuition is like a muscle; the more you develop and train it, the stronger it will be.

Just as it's *technically* possible for all of us to have six-pack abs if we were to dedicate ourselves to strengthening our core, all of us have the potential to be intuitive channels if we dedicate ourselves to practicing. Don't worry, developing your sixth sense is much easier than getting six-pack abs, I promise!

Tapping into our intuition helps us receive guidance from beautiful spirits like angels, fairies, and mermaids. Yes, they're all *real* and divine beings who can generously help us bring more love and joy into our lives. Their wisdom is invaluable as they push us to see what's been holding us back and how we can make significant changes to live the magical life they *know* we can create.

I created this book as your ultimate guide to align your mindset and connect with the angels, fairies, and mermaids to help you manifest the true love you've been dreaming of.

If it's possible for me, just know it's absolutely possible for you! The energy field we live in does not play favorites. We're all equal, so what's possible for one is possible for all. I was able to become an energetic match for romantic love by creating my own manifestation methods, all of which I am going to share with you in this book.

Think of this book as your essential companion filled with exercises, meditations, manifestation rituals, mindset shifts, and enlightened advice to support you on your journey to find love.

Know that it doesn't matter how new or experienced you are with manifesting and connecting to Spirit. You are incredibly capable of tapping into your intuitive senses, connecting with the angels, fairies, and mermaids, and aligning your energy to finally manifest your true love and ideal love story.

As a being in the earthly realm, in order to bring your manifestations to life, it's important for you to take physical action, do the exercises in this book, and dedicate yourself to implementing whatever advice resonates with you. Keep an open mind and try; otherwise, nothing may change. Everything within this book is meant to help you grow.

Most of the exercises include meditation. Meditation is an amazing technique to bring forth clarity and deepen your connection with Spirit. Before starting any meditation, I recommend getting into a quiet, comfortable space where you will not be disturbed. Feel free to sit up or lie down, whatever suits you best. Use essential oils (like lavender for calming) or turn on fairy lights to set the mood. You can find audio versions of my meditations ready to listen to through the QR codes provided in this book.

As you move forward on your journey of manifesting love, you must not try to manifest a specific person. Please do not attempt to re-manifest your ex, your crush (whether you know them, or not), or even a celebrity. It's highly unethical and against another's free will. Think about it—you wouldn't want someone to try to bend energy to make *you* fall in love with them without consent, right? So please don't do this. Honestly, even if you were to try, it wouldn't work. We cannot manifest for another's heart, just as someone cannot manifest for ours.

Manifesting love is not about using magic to force someone to fall in love with you. It's about you, yourself, adjusting the energy you are projecting in order to match the energy of whoever out there would be your perfect partner. It's about getting into alignment with the type of love you deserve and desire.

Leave all your love intentions open to whoever is for your highest good. If you're too busy focusing on one specific person, you will be blocking yourself from the mysterious magic of the Universe. You could be energetically pushing away someone you haven't even met yet, someone who may be the person of your dreams, and who thinks you're the most amazing soul. When it comes to love, the Universe, angels, fairies, and mermaids all know better than we do. So please, ethically manifest and direct all your intentions toward whoever is divinely meant for you.

While I come from the perspective of a heterosexual woman in relationships, the advice within this book can be applied to anyone of any gender expression looking for love in any form because all forms of love are beautiful and supported by the Universe. As we go through each of these exercises, I'll be inclusively using the pronoun 'they' to refer to your incoming true love. Feel free to replace the pronoun as you read with whichever one(s) fits your preference.

Finally, as always, take what resonates with you and leave what doesn't. Manifesting and intuition are all about listening to your own internal guidance system and trusting what feels right to *you*. Follow the practices and exercises from this book that feel most aligned with you.

Now get ready to dive into the magic of working with the angels, fairies, and mermaids to manifest your true love.

You deserve (and have always deserved) your magical ever after in love.

Magical Spirits

Our world is so much more than most people realize. Magic is available to all of us if only we have the courage to believe and simply *ask*.

One of the biggest blessings in my life has been working with Spirit, specifically my angels, mermaids, and fairies. They have helped me in an infinite number of ways, especially with manifesting the most amazing love story.

Here on Earth, we often feel as if we're alone and have to solve every problem by ourselves. We even feel that certain problems can't be solved at all, but the truth is we have mystical helpers available to each of us at all times. In the same way that Cinderella has her fairy godmother, you, too, can receive a magical helping hand.

Yes, the fairy tales you read growing up are absolutely real. Angels, mermaids, and fairies are vibrational beings with the ability to help you call in your happily ever after, and I'm going to show you how to work with each of them.

Before we dive into our mindset shifts and manifestation practices for love, I want to spend time introducing you to the magical entities who will be your guides. Their magic, along with exercises to work with each of them, will be integrated throughout this book. However, first and foremost, it's important to know who exactly they are.

ANGELS

So, first up, we have the angels.

Angels are divine beings born of the highest vibration of pure love. As the ultimate protectors of humankind, they have been tasked with helping make our experiences here on Earth just a little bit easier.

I absolutely love working with angel energy; it was the first energy I was introduced to. When I was 16 years old, I attended the coolest birthday party I had ever been invited to. My friend's mom and grandma were both talented intuitives, so her party involved the two of them giving us all readings, showing us how to work with pendulums, and teaching us how to use angel cards. Most importantly, they told us intuition was a gift within each of us. I remember her grandma specifically telling us that she wasn't born psychic; it was something she developed over time.

As someone who had long dreamed of being able to see the future and cast spells with my fingertip, that was all I needed to hear. From then on, my friend (who was also at the party) and I committed to developing our intuition by practicing reading cards for each other and calling upon the angels for guidance.

On Saturday nights, while other high schoolers were attending parties, we were in her room, doing guided meditations to meet our angels—and I wouldn't have had it any other way!

Even after college, when I began attending intuition development classes, the angels always came through strongly and quickly with the most beautiful guidance. Talking to them was like a form of therapy; it helped me tremendously as I navigated the ups, downs, and uncertainties of my life in my 20s.

While I began this work officially as a teenager, my connection with the angels goes even further back.

When I was 6 years old, I broke my arm in the school playground. The break was right above my elbow and had just missed hitting a growth plate, which could have been serious trouble for my still-growing arm. After surgery and weeks in a cast, my arm was completely fine. I would go on to have two equally strong arms and even become a talented competitive swimmer (if I do say so myself).

By some miraculous luck, I was saved from a bad break, and my mom had told me it was thanks to my guardian angel. She explained that we all have angels that watch over us, and while we can't physically see them, they are always there and doing their best to protect us in any way they can.

While I was still in the hospital recovering from my surgery, my parents and sister brought me my favorite baby doll from home to help me feel better; however, she was freshly adorned with a new guardian angel pin set with a sapphire gem, my birthstone.

From that moment on, I loved angels. I loved knowing I had this ethereal figure always watching over me, protecting me, and even listening to me when I needed someone to talk to.

Being introduced to that concept at such a young age set me up to believe more deeply in the things we can't see and know that this world has a magical element to it.

I've found a lot of people turn off from working with angels because they see them as religious figures stemming from specific belief systems. While different religions across the world do indeed speak of angels delivering messages and guiding prophets, angels are nondenominational. They are not tied to a specific belief system and will work with anyone regardless of their religious and spiritual beliefs. As long as you want to work with angels, they'll want to work with you. It's as simple as that. Angels are open and available to all of us, so long as we ask for help with the purest intentions, of course.

Since angels are beings of the highest light, they don't experience human emotions like we do. Take ease in knowing that they are not going to judge you; they are not going to think you are not worthy enough to work with them; and, they especially are not going to think you are bothering them. In almost every class on angels I've taught, I've encountered students who think the angels are going to consider them a nuisance if they ask for help with every little thing. I promise you are *not* a bother to them! They do not feel those emotions of impatience or annoyance. They *want* you to ask for assistance. Honestly, angels often don't even know what you want help with, nor can they interfere unless you ask, so ask! They are excitedly waiting for you to call upon them.

The only way angels can get involved without your query is if there is a potential situation that is not supposed to be a part of your path. If this is the case, they will subtly intervene to try to nudge you in the right direction. Angels communicate with you via your intuition. It will seem like a random thought that just popped into your head or a gut feeling about which choice to make. While they try to guide us, angels can't control our actions; human free will is very much a thing, so there's no guarantee of their nudges being listened to.

For example, say you were running late on your way out, only to be stuck behind a slow driver on a one-way street. Because of this frustration, you felt an inner nudge to turn and take a different route. Only later, after arriving safely at your destination, did you learn there was a multi-car fender bender on the road you were originally going to take. If you had not been delayed and rerouted, you might've been a part of it. The angels interfered by adding in the lateness and slow driver to intuitively nudge you to take a different route because you were not supposed to be a part of that car accident. In fact, you needed to get to your destination because it was the night you wound up meeting the love of your life!

Certain events need to happen to align with the divine course of the Universe's will. Alternatively in the case above, maybe you felt an intuitive nudge to be patient and continue on that original route. Maybe the angels sent you that way because you needed to be in that fender bender because one of the other drivers involved would wind up becoming your future spouse!

As for my broken arm, the angels couldn't have prevented it from breaking entirely, as that event led me to believe in angels. However, they helped ease the severity of the break because having my arm heal completely was important for major chapters of my life path later on. I needed to become a competitive swimmer as it taught me about perseverance, mindset, and even manifesting. Some of my first intentional manifestations occurred in the pool, as I realized that when I visualized myself winning a race, I would. Being on the swim team in high school is also where I became friends with the girls who would lead me to that fateful psychic party that changed my life.

Sometimes unfortunate things may happen, and you may wonder, "*Well, why didn't the angels help there?*" Life exists in polarity. We're always going to have a mix of both good and bad. Some things are just inexplicable or outright unfair. In certain cases, for your own growth, you can try to see a deeper lesson. Perhaps that unfortunate event pushed you to make changes and go down a new path, a better path. Maybe part of that path is to help others avoid the hardship you experienced.

Our souls incarnate for a reason. 'Earth School' is not easy, and none of us are immune to arduous challenges. These challenges are essential for our personal growth and for the growth of humanity as a whole. The angels can't interfere by eliminating our lessons entirely; however, they will do their best to help us understand the lessons, heal our hearts, and feel the light.

Keep in mind that while the Universe's plan will always outweigh everything else, you can still ask the angels for help every day in every way with anything you'd like! Every single time I have a problem, my go-to is to call upon my angels to help me find a solution. It works just like magic.

I've asked them for help fixing my seemingly broken laptop, for all green lights when I'm running just a few minutes late to work, and, of course, for guidance aligning myself with attracting true love.

When it comes to angels, there are two main types that I recommend working with.

GUARDIAN ANGELS

As I mentioned earlier, we have our own guardian angels, a group of beings who watch over us. Guardian angels can be a mix of loved ones on the other side, ancestors, or our spirit guides. Spirit guides are specific ethereal beings whose purpose is dedicated to helping us stick to our life path. They know us, our hopes, and our dreams better than anyone. They're with us before life as we plan our incarnation and stay with us all the way until we reach the other side, where they'll help us conduct our life review.

While guardian angels aren't the focus of this book, it's important to know you have your own personal team of spirit guides offering gentle guidance and protection.

ARCHANGELS

The main type of angel you will be working with in this book are archangels.

I like to compare archangels to the ancient gods and goddesses. Just as the Greeks had Aphrodite to help with love and the Egyptians had Thoth to help with writing, the archangels each have their own names and areas of expertise. They are beings we can pray to or call upon anytime we'd like. While guardian angels are specific to each individual, the same archangels are available to everyone.

Archangels can be everywhere all at once, so multiple people across the globe can reach out to them, and they will have the time and ability to hear and help everyone.

Archangels also have no set gender. They are fluid beings and exist in multiple forms, which means sometimes you may receive the masculine version of an angel, sometimes the feminine version, and sometimes a non-binary version.

I have always received Archangel Gabriel in the masculine form; however, in many oracle decks, Gabriel is often depicted in the feminine form. Neither is right or wrong; as with everything in nature, there is a balance of gendered energies.

Noticing the form your archangel appears will add an extra layer to your message. If you receive an angel in the feminine form, it indicates you need to tap more into the art of surrendering and use your divine intuition. If an angel shows up in the masculine form, they're encouraging you to take a more action-oriented approach. If an angel shows up as non-binary, you need to balance both energies: go with the flow *and* take action!

There are dozens of archangels, some more well-known than others, but for the purposes of manifesting love, there are six specific ones we will be working with.

Chamuel

First, there's Archangel Chamuel. Chamuel is one of my favorite angels to work with and has a light blue and light pink aura. Chamuel helps you find whatever you are looking for. This can be in your search for love but also for smaller tasks like helping you find missing personal items. I once lost my sunglasses for weeks at the beginning of spring. I finally remembered to ask Chamuel and heard "in your winter coat pocket" pop into my head. I went over to look in my winter coat that I hadn't worn in weeks, and, sure enough, there they were in that exact pocket!

Chamuel is considered one of the romance angels as they specifically help us find soulmate love. I once made a list of all the qualities I wanted my true love to have and asked Chamuel to help me find someone as close to that list as possible. It wasn't long after that I was led to my true love (who matched my list almost entirely, even down to the minor things like the sports he played and movies he liked).

Jophiel

Next is Archangel Jophiel. Jophiel has a magenta-pink aura and is the archangel of beauty. She helps us romanticize our lives and fall in love with our journeys. Another romance angel, Jophiel, is fantastic at helping us see the beauty in ourselves, both inside and out. She also helps us physically manifest beauty. Yes, you can ask Jophiel for a good hair day on your next date. Nothing is too silly or superfluous for her. She is happy to help make you happy. I have definitely asked Jophiel for help looking my best on many occasions—including my wedding day.

Michael

The next angel is one you may have heard of: Archangel

Michael. Archangel Michael has a purple, navy blue, and gold aura, and is the archangel of protection. When dating, it's great to ask Michael to protect you from whoever is not for your highest good. After making that declaration, you may find your date canceling or not asking for a second date. This would be an ideal time to remind yourself that while it may sting, it's just Archangel Michael saving you from a disaster down the line. After asking for Michael's help, if the date goes well, you know you have Michael's approval.

Archangel Michael is also excellent for cleansing our energy and helping us release negativity from our past. We'll be working with Michael to release our romantic past so we can move forward confidently.

Raziel

Along with Michael, Archangel Raziel is great to work with to release our past—*past lifetimes*, that is. Archangel Raziel has a rainbow aura, and they help us unlock the mysteries of our previous incarnations. Sometimes, no matter how much healing, manifesting, and journaling we do, we have certain blocks that we continually struggle to break free of. If that's the case, the answer to what's blocking us may lie, not in this lifetime but beyond, in our past lives. Deep within our subconscious minds, we store all the experiences we've ever had. A negative romantic experience from a previous lifetime can carry over energetically into this lifetime and continue to affect us. This is why it's important to connect with Archangel Raziel to understand what happened and finally heal that part of yourself so you can move forward in love block-free.

Haniel

Archangel Haniel is the archangel of divine feminine energy. She is closely associated with the moon and her aura is a pale moonlight blue. Haniel helps us strengthen and listen to our intuition. She also helps us practice surrendering to the will of the Universe, which is so incredibly important when it comes to manifesting love.

Raphael

Finally, we have Archangel Raphael, another well-known archangel you may have heard of. With his green aura, Raphael is the archangel of healing. Giving yourself permission to be vulnerable and heal is one of the most important steps to aligning yourself with love. Surrounding yourself with Raphael's healing green aura will assist you in resetting your energy and is a visualization practice you can do daily.

Keep these six archangels in mind as we will be working with them all to help you manifest the love story of your dreams. Love is the highest energetic vibration. When soulmates find each other, that unification adds beautiful loving energy to the collective frequency of the Earth. This boosts the vibration of the entire planet. Since the archangels are made of pure love themselves, *of course,* they want to help you and your true love find each other!

Scan the QR code to download and listen to the audio version of this meditation found at the back of this book.

A Meditation to Introduce Yourself to an Archangel

Take a deep breath in and a deep breath out.

Take a deep breath in and a deep breath out.

Imagine a beautiful beam of white light coming down from the divine and into your crown chakra, located at the top of your head.

The white light fills your crown chakra, cleansing and clearing every inch of it as the beam becomes a bridge, a connection between you and your angels.

The white light travels down your forehead and opens your third eye chakra, cleansing and clearing every inch of it, allowing you to clearly see your angels.

The white light travels down to your ears, opening them, clearing away any interference, and allowing you to clearly hear your angels.

The white light travels down to your throat chakra, cleansing and clearing every inch of it, opening it wider and wider, allowing you to clearly communicate with your angels.

The white light travels down to your heart chakra, cleansing and clearing every inch of it, allowing you to feel the radiant love your angels have for you and the radiant love you deserve in this lifetime and all your lifetimes.

The white light travels down to your solar plexus chakra, cleansing and clearing every inch of it, allowing you to trust your instincts, your gut feelings, and that everything you are intuitively experiencing is real.

The white light travels down to your sacral chakra, cleansing and clearing every inch of it, filling you with brilliant solutions and new ideas, as you are now an open, creative channel.

Finally, the white light travels down to your root chakra, cleansing and clearing every inch of it and grounding you to the beautiful, divine Mother Earth.

You are now filled top to bottom with beautiful white light.

You are now a clear and open channel.

You are now ready to speak to your angels.

You are safe. You are protected. You are only available to talk to spirits of the highest level of light and love with the purest intentions of all involved.

Now, take a moment to call upon a specific archangel of your choosing or ask for whichever archangel is with you to please step forward.

As the archangel comes to you, take in their appearance, note their aura color, what they look like, and most importantly, see how divine their energy feels.

Once they are with you, introduce yourself to them and ask them to share any wisdom that could guide you on your journey right now, specifically about your love life, if you so wish.

Once you've asked, listen and allow your conversation with them to go on for as long as you need.

When you're finished, thank them for all their help and guidance, send them divine love, and know you can continue to connect with them whenever you wish.

Feel free to journal about your experience connecting to the archangels.

ELEMENTALS

While angels exist in the ultra-high vibrational angelic realm and have to lower their frequency to interact with us here on the Earth plane, our next two groups of divine beings—mermaids and fairies—come to us directly from the Earth plane, specifically from the elemental realm.

Just as some people may be hesitant to work with angels, seeing them as too religious, others may be hesitant to work with mermaids and fairies as they believe them to be fictitious.

The truth is they're actually real.

Legend has it long ago before the world was so crowded and industrialized, we could see almost all those beings we now believe to be that of myth. Dragons, unicorns, leprechauns, mermaids, and fairies all walked among us. However, as the hunt against magic began, and those deemed magical were persecuted, these beings faded from being easily seen in our dimension to protect themselves. However, they still watch over the Earth from a separate dimension, and their magic continues to be available to help those pure of heart, who believe, and have respect for our planet. Elementals' main purpose is to help our Earth thrive. As you are part of the Earth, this help is also extended to you.

They are called elementals as they derive from the four classical elements—air, water, fire, and earth. Elementals have duties to purify and improve our natural planet. Like the angels, they vibrate at a higher frequency than we humans, though at times, elementals will slow themselves down to communicate with us. They even show their presence to a lucky few.

When working with spirits in general, elementals and angels included, it is important to maintain your boundaries and practice good energetic hygiene. This is especially important when working with elementals, as their first allegiance is to the Earth, not specifically or only to humanity. Surround yourself in a bubble of light and declare you are only available to work with spirits of the highest level of light and love with the purest intentions for all involved. You can even call in Archangel Michael to stay by your side and guard you further. If you ever feel uneasy and sense you have connected with an elemental who is not aligned with your intentions, disconnect immediately. Declare the spirit must leave and call upon Archangel Michael to protect you. Visualize bringing white light into your space and into your body, dissolving away any negativity.

Please do not let this deter you from working with elementals. So long as you properly protect yourself, as described above, and treat the elementals with the utmost respect, you will be safe. Elementals are beautiful spirits who have tremendous wisdom. Their close vibrational relationship with the Earth realm makes them indispensable allies for manifestation. Working with them can help you tap into magic on a whole new level.

I adore working with the mermaids (water elementals) and fairies (air elementals) for manifesting love as they each bring their own unique magic and vibrant divinity.

Mermaids

As water elementals, mermaids help us better understand our deep emotional nature. They encourage us not to be afraid to put ourselves out there and wear our hearts on our sleeves. Mermaids (who also present as mermen and mer-beings) help connect us with our deep, sensual, and romantic side.

As divine entities of the sea, they love *love* and want to show you how to swim after your heart's wishes. They also teach you to be like the ocean and surrender to the ebbs and flows of life, understanding that everything, even love, exists in cyclical balance.

The mermaids are masters of romance, so not only can they help you manifest love in the first place, but they also can help you sustain romance throughout your entire lifetime. Think of them as wise older siblings who always have spot-on advice for your love life.

Communicating with the mermaids regularly helps you develop a friendship with them, as they guide you toward all the life-long romance you desire.

As with all elementals, it is recommended that you offer a gift in exchange for their help. This isn't a payment (payments usually offend elementals), it's a kind gesture to show them gratitude. For the mermaids, you can either present them with gifts in your mind as you speak with them (gifting them treasures, treats, or pearls), or you can offer the gift of assisting with ocean conservation. Safely picking up litter on your local beach or donating to charities that help clean the oceans and heal marine life would be wonderful gifts to the mermaids, who do so much to preserve our waters.

While I am fortunate to have grown up on the south shore of Long Island, just a few miles from the Atlantic Ocean, and have been able to connect with the mermaids there, it's not a problem if you don't live near an ocean. While going to the beach is the best place to meditate and connect with the mermaids, you can connect with them from anywhere, even in a landlocked state or country.

All you have to do is picture the ocean in your mind's eye, add salt to your bath, or surround yourself with ocean items like seashells. Anything sea-related is perfect to invoke their energy. Just like the angels, if you are pure of heart and want to work with the mermaids, they'll respond to you.

Mermaids are excellent companions on the road to manifesting and maintaining love, and I know you are going to love working with their magic!

Scan the QR code to download and listen to the audio version of this meditation found at the back of this book.

A Meditation to Introduce Yourself to Mermaids

Take a deep breath in and a deep breath out.

Take a deep breath in and a deep breath out.

Visualize yourself standing on the most beautiful beach. Feel the soft, warm sand between your toes. Hear the seagulls and the sound of waves gently swirling in and out.

Maybe you see palm trees, maybe it's a beach full of seashells, maybe it's sunrise, maybe it's sunset; just trust whatever is coming to you.

Above all, see the beautiful, mighty ocean before you. Feel overflowing gratitude for this stunning marvel of nature.

Know you are safe. You are protected, and you will only interact with mermaids of the highest level of light with the purest intentions of love for all involved.

Now, reach out with your energy into the ocean. Extend your gratitude deeply into the depths of the beautiful sea. Continue to feel grateful and know you are connecting with the most magical mermaids of the highest level of light and love.

As your gratitude reaches the beautiful mysterious depths of the ocean, you may see shimmering coral reefs, you may see beautiful fish, you may see an underwater mermaid city, or you may see ocean blue. Just know anything you see is okay. It's all safe; you are safe.

Now, ask for any pure-intentioned mermaids who wish to work with you and who have divine messages for you today, to please swim forward to meet you.

Wait and see as a mermaid swims into your presence.

Take in what you see. What do they look like? What color are their fins and tail? How does their energy feel?

Firstly, introduce yourself and thank this mermaid for all they do to help the ocean and the world. Then offer them a gift as a form of gratitude—maybe it's a piece of treasure, a pearl, a treat. See something meaningful appear in your hands and offer it to your mermaid.

Introduce yourself and ask what guidance they wish to share with you, perhaps specifically around your love life.

Listen to them and proceed to have a full conversation with your mermaid. You can ask them to show you what is important for your next steps or just any wisdom they feel inclined share with you today.

Let this conversation go on for as long as you wish.

Once you've finished the conversation, deeply thank your mermaid for introducing themselves, and thank them for all they've done for you, all the wisdom and blessings they've shared.

Send them divine love, and know you can continue to connect with them whenever you wish.

Feel free journal about your experience connecting to the mermaids.

Fairies

Finally, our third group of companions we'll connect with on our manifesting journey are the fairies: air elementals.

I think fairies often get a bad reputation, and some people are afraid to work with them as they can be seen as tricky—think Puck in *A Midsummer Night's Dream* (which is, no surprise, my favorite play of all time). However, as with working with any spirit, as long as you set the intention to work with fairies of the purest intentions and of the most divine light, you will only receive those types of fairies to help you.

There is nothing to be afraid of. Fairy energy is magical, exuberant, and maybe a bit mischievous, but in a fun, sassy way. Anytime I've connected with fairies, I have always interacted with the absolute sweetest beings. They are beyond kind, super encouraging, and helpful. Some of them are serious but some are also silly. They'll tell it like it is and may call you out but, by being upfront and honest, they'll provide you with exactly what you need.

While fairies overall are considered air elementals, there are subclassifications of fairies with each of the four elements. There are flower fairies (earth) whose main purpose is to assist with the purification of soil and growing flowers and plants. Salamanders (fire) bring the spark of fire into our world and sylphs (air) who purify the air we breathe. Some of my favorites to work with are ice fairies (water) who help us learn to slow down and work with the magic of winter. We'll be working more with the element-specific fairies in this book, including the flower fairies, salamanders, and sylphs. Though we won't be working with the ice fairies directly, they want to share their message of patience and remind you that it is okay to take your time as you work to manifest both self-love and romantic love. Love takes time to thaw and the only way to melt is to shine your brightest light.

Fairies are wonderful at helping us with love because they, like the mermaids, adore romance. Their vibe is all about having fun. While they have duties such as purifying the air and helping the flowers grow, their favorite activities are dancing, playing, and enjoying existence. Fairies can teach us to do the same, to see life as something to enjoy and prioritize fun. When we do that, we align our energy to manifest even more joy and wonder.

Keep in mind that manifestations happen instantly in the elemental realm. Here in the human realm, our manifestations take some time and require divine patience. Working with the fairies can help you embody their instant-manifestation energy to remind yourself the second you ask—the moment you put out a thought, a feeling, a wish—the best thing you can do is act as if it's already here. Pretend your wish has been granted; it's already manifested for you! There is power in that.

Just like the mermaids, it's best to present the fairies with a gift; not as payment but as a token of gratitude. Fairies love shiny items, jewelry, crystals, and treats such as chocolate, milk, and honey. One time, my husband participated in a class I was teaching about fairies, and in the meditation, he felt called to present them with a big, gold leaf. He said the fairies adored it and thought it was an exceptional offering.

You can present your gift to them in your mind's eye or leave out crystals or treats dedicated to them. Fairies will enjoy the treats via their energy, so if you physically leave treats for them, wait a few days, ask the fairies if they are finished with it, and if you feel a "yes" then you know it is safe to discard.

Scan the QR code to download and listen to the audio version of this meditation found at the back of this book.

A Meditation to Introduce Yourself to Fairies

Take a deep breath in and a deep breath out.

Take a deep breath in and a deep breath out.

Imagine yourself walking barefoot through a beautiful forest.

It might be nighttime or a beautiful sunny day. Either way, this forest is twinkling.

The wind blows through your hair. You notice an abundance of wild overgrown flowers, strong, sturdy trees, and a babbling brook.

This place makes you feel happy and incredibly safe.

You keep walking until you find a beautiful spot to rest. Maybe it's next to a mighty tree, near a stream, or surrounded by more flowers. Trust what you are seeing.

Find somewhere comfortable to sit in this beautiful place, and take a deep breath in and a deep breath out.

From your pocket, you take out a beautiful little gift. Maybe it's milk and honey, maybe it's chocolate, maybe it's something shiny like jewelry.

Whatever it is, trust that it will be gratefully received and place it in front of you. Offer it as a gift.

Now that you've made your offering, ask that any benevolent fairies of the highest level of light and love with pure intentions be with you now.

Wait and see, as fairies appear. Take in their appearance and experience their energy.

Thank them for being with you today and tell them you are excited to work with them and develop a magical connection.

Now, introduce yourself and ask them to share any wisdom or advice they wish to share with you, perhaps even specifically around your love life.

Allow this conversation to go on for as long as you need.

When you're finished, thank them for all their help and guidance, send them divine love, and know you can continue to connect with them whenever you wish.

Feel free to journal about your experience connecting to the fairies.

Those are your guides—the angels, mermaids, and fairies—all beautiful, divine beings who are happy to help you. Throughout the rest of this book, we'll get deeper into our mindset around love, healing our past, and loving ourselves.

Exercises will be sprinkled throughout to work with all these amazing entities to manifest your dream romance. Now that you've practiced introducing yourself to all of them, you'll have a better sense of working with them to create your magical ever after.

Your Love Mindset

Take a moment right now to make a list (physical or mental) and consider all your current thoughts about dating, your romantic life, and just love in general.

Did you do it? Great.

Now, reflect upon your list, and ask yourself: How does this align with what I've been experiencing in love?

It's probably an exact match, right? But the first question wasn't asking what you were experiencing; it was just asking about your thoughts. So, can you clearly see that your thoughts align with your reality? This brings us to the basic principle of understanding manifestation: *your thoughts create your reality.*

Becoming aware of my thoughts and changing them was the best thing I ever could've done. It truly altered my life, especially in love. Sometimes, it can be hard to face that we've been the problem, fueling the cycle of what we don't want. We *need* to call ourselves out! It's the only way we're going to evolve. My game-changer was realizing my thoughts had become "I never meet anyone good to date" on a loop.

The Universe is always listening and it perceives your thoughts as commands. When you say, "There's no one good to date," the Universe believes *you want that* and will give it to you. We live in a giant energy field, and whatever energy *you* project into it must come back to you. Because I was constantly thinking there was no one good to date, the Universe picked up on my energy and was manifesting that for me, and I was indeed experiencing *no one good to date.*

Wild, right? It's also incredibly helpful because if you are now realizing you have been unintentionally calling in what you don't want, it also means you have the power to call in *exactly what you do want!*

For me, everything changed when I became aware of all my negative thoughts about love. Anytime I found myself wanting to internally rant about feeling hopeless about dating, frustrated about not meeting anyone, or annoyed that I'd only meet people who wanted casual hook-ups and not the serious commitment I wanted—I caught myself.

I would then pause my spiraling and note to my brain that those were unhelpful and untrue thoughts, and I would choose to believe the opposite. I would instantly affirm in my head: *It is easy for me to meet good potential people to date. There are loyal people who want romance and a serious, committed relationship. I am lucky in love! I am loved. I am in love. Dating is fun and easy! My love life is thriving!*

An online trend said, "The solulu is to be delulu," slang for "The solution is to be delusional." That's exactly what you need to do here. Pretend. Be "delusional." No one will read your thoughts—except the Universe, and it doesn't judge; it just accepts your thoughts as is and wants to bring them to you. The more you make it feel real in your head, the more it *has* to manifest into your reality. Feel your feelings *always*—your emotions are important—but when you're ready, let go of unhelpful thoughts and start to play pretend.

As you're getting dressed up to meet your friends, pretend you're getting ready for a date. As you're driving to work, pretend you're driving to see the love of your life. When you pick up your phone to check social media, pretend it's because you just saw an "I love you!" text pop up from your partner. You can even text yourself "I love you" to not only get yourself into the energy of being someone who sends "I love you" texts, but also into the energy of receiving them. Whenever you text yourself, the same message instantly returns back to you. When you see this "I love you" text return, pretend it's from your partner. It may seem silly, but no one has to know you're doing this, and if it helps you get into that happy-in-love energy, why not?

Instead of being sad around Valentine's Day, browse stores as if you are picking out a gift for your partner. Scroll through travel sites and pretend you're booking a romantic vacation for the two of you. Get excited! Feel the love in your heart *now*. Believe wholeheartedly that you have it *already*.

It may take some time to get yourself used to thinking positively, but the more you catch your unhelpful thoughts and replace them with better ones, the easier it becomes. Eventually, this new way of thinking will feel natural. Right now, your brain is so used to thinking love never works out for you that it automatically follows those unhelpful thought patterns. By consciously shifting your thoughts, you begin the process of rewiring your mind to align with your dream love life.

This doesn't mean shutting out all negativity. As humans, we are meant to feel the full spectrum of emotions, and you should allow yourself to feel all your feelings rather than bottling them up or pushing them aside. Committing yourself to this mindset shift doesn't mean you won't ever have a negative thought—it means you won't let the negative thoughts control or define you. Instead, you'll be in charge, guiding your thoughts toward the love and happiness you truly deserve.

FEELINGS RANT

Of course, you never want to bottle up your negative feelings. You want to fully feel them in order to heal them. One thing that helps me process and move through my emotions (rather than just push the bad ones away) is to go on what I call a *feelings rant.*

I developed this method in college when I lived in the city. I would give myself ten blocks of walking to internally feel and express everything negative to give a voice to what wasn't serving me, and get it out of my system.

Years later when I had moved back to the suburbs and was not walking blocks, I switched to setting a timer for five minutes. This is a method I still do all the time, and it feels so good afterward. In the set time, I'll allow myself the full duration to rant about anything and everything that's currently bothering me, everything that's wrong about life.

I want you to do this! Use this dedicated time to release all your dating frustrations, annoyance at your exes, and any depleting feelings about love. When you give a voice to your harsher feelings of anger or sadness, you uncork that bottle. You can set it free and get it out of your system and out of your energy field. You *prevent it* from manifesting because it will no longer be stewing within you.

Rant for the full duration. If time or blocks are left still and you think you're finished, *keep going*. Pick out all the petty little things that bother you—including the things that are so minuscule compared to your bigger problems that they might even make you laugh! I guarantee getting all of this out of your system will help you feel better; way better than if you tried to suppress or ignore your negative feelings.

Once the timer has gone off or you've reached the end of your walking distance, shake out your feelings—literally. Shake out your entire body and use your hands to sweep and dust any bad vibes off you.

Call upon your archangels to help remove that negativity and imagine beautiful rainbow light surrounding and healing you. Ask Archangel Michael to release any negativity around you, Archangel Raphael to heal your thoughts, and Archangel Jophiel to help you see the beauty already in your life.

After that, set another timer or declare another walking marker for double your original time or distance. If you set your timer for 5 minutes on the first round, set this duration for 10 minutes. If you walked 10 blocks last time, go for 20 this time. Now it's time to go on a gratitude spree and *positively* rant about all the things you love about life. Think about all the people, places, and things you're grateful for. Connect with everything that makes you happy. Maybe even feel excited knowing that your love problems are already solved.

When the timer is done, thank your angels for being with you, and ask them to deliver those good vibes directly to the Universe to come back to you manifested.

SOCIAL AMPLIFICATION

You have the power to create your reality. Sure, hard things and hard times may have happened, and most of them may have been out of your control, but those things don't have to define you. They don't have to continue to hold you back and certainly don't make you unworthy of having a happily ever after. Life is cyclic; we will all face hard times, but we can't let them stop us from claiming our internal power and creating a magical life.

Just because you've had hardships in love doesn't mean you're doomed to experience those continually. Happiness is possible for you. You deserve it. True love can *(and will)* happen for you and be better than you ever expected.

It's also helpful to watch how you speak about love, not only within your inner monologue but to everyone else in your life. It's one thing to hold uplifting thoughts in your mind, but can you embody these new beliefs when speaking with your friends?

This was another game-changer for me. While I'd set all these positive intentions and declarations about love in my head, I was *still* slinking back into my negativity about dating when chatting with my friends. Collectively, we'd complain about love and feed into that hopeless energy. Because the words we speak have power, those disempowering words and feelings were *undoing* the positive affirmations or manifestations I had been trying to commit to.

The Universe needs you to be *fully committed to believing*. If you are talking to your friends, your family, your co-workers, or your hairdresser about how hard love is for you that means you *do not fully believe*. Sure, it can be difficult because it's your current truth, right? Obviously, you don't want to lie.

To help me stay committed to showing the Universe that I fully believed, I shifted my conversations toward telling my friends that I felt hopeful about love. I knew it had to work out eventually, and true love would come for them, too. I'd listen to their complaints because people need to be heard, but in my head, I'd affirm: *Love is easy. Love is here for me. I have love. My friends have love, too.*

Talk more about what it will be like when it all works out. You can try changing the subject to something more uplifting, which will energetically help everyone involved.

Try *not* to take love advice from unhappily single friends. Just as you wouldn't take money advice from someone who's broke, cooking advice from someone who's never held a frying pan, nor serious medical advice from someone who's not a doctor—don't take love advice from those who aren't happily in love themselves!

One helpful thing I did when I was single was ask one of my best friends who was with her true love, the man who soon became her husband, what it felt like to be with the person you know is "the one." A massive smile stretched across her face, and she said, "It's the best." She went on to tell me how they can never get enough of each other and that he makes her so incredibly happy.

Rather than listen to the bitter, single people in my life who told me my standards were too high and I was delusional for thinking someday my Prince Charming would come, I took my friend's words to heart and tapped into the feelings she described, knowing if she could be over the moon in love, I could be too.

Try to avoid sharing memes that joke about being single forever.

Don't feed into that internet culture of self-deprecating humor because, you guessed it, that *too* gets picked up by the energy field of the Universe, and will further cement love not working out.

Think of it this way—if you already had the love of your life and were happily in the romance of your dreams with "the one," would you share posts about how frustrating love is or how terrible people are? No. Would you be complaining to your friends and family? No. Would you be thinking about how love is the worst? Would you be feeling jealous when you see other couples? Also, no. Would you be worried about *when* meeting "the one" will happen? Or how much others are judging you if you haven't met them yet? Still no.

You wouldn't be stressing about any of that! You'd be happy. You'd feel secure, safe, and joyous. You'd celebrate other couples. You'd celebrate yourself. You'd talk positively about your partner to others, encourage your single friends who want love, and you certainly wouldn't be worried about timelines.

The key to manifesting anything is embodying the version of you that has it *now*.

Technically, time doesn't exist. Everything that has ever happened and will ever happen coexists all at once. The Universe only knows one moment, and it's the present.

When your thoughts dwell on reliving the hardships of the past or stressing about the future, the Universe doesn't interpret it as a different time; it only sees it as if you are experiencing it right now. Thus, it's going to bring you *more of that*.

Step into the version of yourself who already has love—think and act as they would—and let go of the worry. By doing this, you tell the Universe that love is already yours, you trust its timing, and you fully believe.

That will make it manifest for you.

You may declare and affirm, "I have love!" or "I'm so happy I'm in love!" and try to visualize it, but if your daily habits and consistent thoughts and feelings don't support a person who is in love, then it's going to be hard for that love to come in.

In a way, aren't we all just playing roles during our time here on Earth? You've been cast as *you* and are the lead actor for this lifetime; now is the scene where you play the part of being your happiest in love.

Now, reflect and ask yourself the following questions:

- ✦ *How would the version of me who is already in love act?*
- ✦ *What would my regular habits be?*
- ✦ *What would my thoughts be?*
- ✦ *How would I react to seeing other couples?*
- ✦ *How would I react to engagement announcements or wedding invites?*
- ✦ *How would I feel on a regular basis?*

For deeper personalized clarity, I love turning to my oracle cards and journaling, specifically working with the mermaids. The prompts in the next exercise will help you better understand what you want and dedicate yourself to shifting your mindset!

ORACLE READING AND JOURNALING WITH THE MERMAIDS

Mermaids are masters at interpreting emotions, so they'll help you understand everything you are feeling and show you how those feelings are manifesting your reality.

In the warmer months, head to the beach with a deck of cards and a journal. If you don't live near a beach or it's a colder season, you can play a scenic beach ambiance video on your TV, set a picture of the beach in front of you, or even play beach sounds. Do anything you can to pretend you're there and find a quiet, peaceful space where you won't be disturbed.

Extend your aura and reach out into the ocean to connect with the mermaids' energy.

You may wish to repeat the 'Meditation to Introduce Yourself to Mermaids' exercise from earlier, and perhaps set the intention to connect with the same mermaids you previously met. As always, thank them for their guidance and ask to interact only with mermaids of the highest level of light with the purest intention for all involved. Present them with a gift (e.g. an aquamarine crystal, a pearl, a trinket, treasure) either in your mind's eye, or as a natural physical object if you're actually at the beach. Please be mindful and don't put anything harmful into the ocean!

Then, ask the mermaids to help you connect with your truest emotions. Be honest with yourself, and respond from the heart.

As you put your pen to paper, answer the following journal prompts. Take your time as you navigate these questions. Some prompts may be more challenging than others, but be patient and give yourself grace. You can complete this exercise all at once, or break it into multiple sessions. If you choose to split the session, make sure to repeat the meditation beforehand.

Letting Go of Negativity

1. If no one else's opinions matter, what does my heart truly want?

2. What negative thoughts about love am I still holding on to?

3. How can I release these negative thoughts, and what thoughts can I replace them with?

Commitment to Your Vision of Love

4. How can I dedicate myself to consistently believing that I deserve love?

5. How can I prove to myself that I am worthy of love?

6. Why do I want love?

Swimming through Challenges to Create Ease and Flow

7. How can I embody the version of me who is in love? What thoughts and habits would I have?

8. What are some past examples of times when things turned out in my favor?

9. If it worked out then, why can't it work out this time, in love?

Embodying Mermaid Wisdom

10. How can I be like the ocean—flowing effortlessly

and trusting everything in my love life is working in my favor?

11. How can I embody mermaid energy and romanticize my entire life?

12. Write about your ideal love life as if you are already experiencing it.

Once you've finished, hold your journal to your heart and infuse those wishes with your loving energy. Thank the mermaids for helping you answer these questions, then move on to your oracle cards.

Hold your deck to your heart, thank the mermaids, and ask them to guide these cards with the most accurate messages possible so you can hear, see, and feel divine guidance. Ask

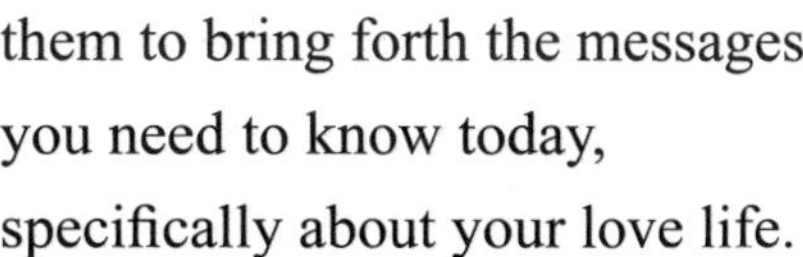

them to bring forth the messages you need to know today, specifically about your love life.

Then shuffle the deck for as long as you feel called to and pull out one to three cards.

Place the cards in front of you and consider the imagery. Ask the mermaids to explain what these cards mean *before* you reach for the guidebook.

Focus on the energy of the cards. Quiet your mind, and trust whatever is coming to you. Tap into all your clair senses: your clairvoyance (clear seeing), clairaudience (clear hearing), clairsentience (clear feeling), and claircognizance (clear knowing). Pay attention to what you are seeing in your mind's eye, hearing, feeling, and just knowing. Use your intuition to receive divine downloads from the mermaids.

Trust your instincts. Trust that the messages popping into your head have come for a reason—

believe in them! I promise you are not making them up.

Feel free to pull more cards if you need to and allow the conversation with the mermaids to go on for as long as you wish.

When you're finished, hold the deck to your heart once more, thank your cards and your mermaids for all their guidance as you send them love and gratitude.

QUESTION SOCIAL TRUISMS

Society fills our brains with so many lies about love: *Love doesn't last. Most marriages end in divorce. If you haven't found the love of your life by a certain age, there's something wrong with you. It's normal to fight all the time. Men always forget anniversaries. Women always nag. Marriage is constant hard work.*

All of these are other people's truths that they likely adopted from previous generations' views of reality. These views come from a medley of things including restrictive social conventions, expectations of gender roles, family dynamics, and unprocessed generational trauma. We can acknowledge previous generations may not have had the opportunity, space, and tools to heal and we can send them compassion. We can also acknowledge that carrying their limiting beliefs with us is unhelpful in creating the future we want to experience.

So many have given in to accepting outdated limiting beliefs about love, and thus, because they believed and *expected* them, they manifested them and continued to solidify them as their truths.

You are never, ever behind in life. It is never too late to find love. Just because it hasn't happened yet doesn't mean it never will.

Remember, just because they're society's truths doesn't mean they have to be *your* truths. Not a single thing that anyone else thinks about love has to be your truth. This is *your* empowered reality; this is your fairy tale. The glitter pen is in your hand, and you can create any story you want.

Society has some weird sentiment that 30 is old, and if you're not married or at least with the love of your life by that age, you're behind. How absolutely ridiculous is that? If a child doesn't start fully walking by 1, you're not going to tell them, *"Oh, it's too late; you missed your window. You're never going to walk; give up forever."* No, you let them keep trying, and eventually, they get it.

Why would you think the same to yourself about finding love? Everyone moves at their own pace in life, especially with love. You are exactly on time, *your* time. Love can happen at any stage because the Universe has its own unique plan for you. You could meet the love of your life when you're 16, 25, 49, or 83. There's no timeline for love; there's no age limit. I can't emphasize enough that *it is never too late!*

There's no wrong or right or expected time to meet them, just as there's no one place you can meet them. Some people meet at work; some people meet at school. Some people meet through friends, some through dating apps, and some through a chance encounter just by being in the same place at the same time—it's all different, and that's the beauty of life. Life is supposed to be filled with variety. We all have our own love stories.

If you're particularly panicked about feeling like you're too old or think you should have met someone by now, please look at examples of amazing souls who started their love stories around your age or even later in life. Find examples of people you may know, look up celebrity couples, or search the internet for love stories of people who got married in their 40s, 50s, 60s—and beyond! Remind yourself that it's perfectly acceptable, and perhaps even preferable, if you don't meet the love of your life in high school or college. It's also surely okay if you're not married or engaged by a certain age. You don't even need to get married at all! It's not a life requirement.

It's also okay if you married young and got divorced, or lost your previous partner through tragic circumstances. It's okay if you've been married multiple times. It's okay if you've been in several long-term relationships that didn't work out. Don't necessarily think of divorce or break-ups as a bad thing either, because these endings just mean you were brave enough to admit what you thought you wanted wasn't what you wanted. Divorce or breakups indicate you were strong enough to choose yourself and choose happiness. Or, if it was your partner who initiated the ending of the relationship, reframe it as the Universe removing someone who didn't value you as much as you deserve in order make space for someone who will! However your previous relationships ended, have the power to initiate a beautiful healing journey that helps you discover your true self.

Meeting the love of your life later in life has absolutely zero reflection on how lovable you are, how attractive you are, and who you are as a person. The only thing it means is that you didn't meet the one yet. You didn't settle. You have standards. You're holding out for the best, and that's admirable.

I was glad I didn't meet the love of my life in high school or college because I wouldn't have been ready for him then. I hadn't learned enough. I didn't love myself enough. I wasn't ready for that kind of commitment, even though I thought I was. Meeting him when I was 25, beginning to date three weeks before I turned 27, getting engaged at 31, and getting married on our dating anniversary just before I turned 33 was the perfect timeline for me—one I felt comfortable with and ready for at each stage.

Reflecting on it now, I *still* feel like that all happened pretty early in life. We met young, even though 20-something me thought I was behind. Silly, right? The Universe always knows when both you and your true love are ready—so just keep trusting that it will happen in divine timing.

Give yourself permission to reject societal beliefs around age and embrace your unique timeline.

The moment you surrender and tell the Universe, "Whatever you want for me, *whenever* you want it for me, is fine!" and genuinely believe it, is usually when it comes together.

My younger self had declared to the Universe, "You know what? If you want me single for the rest of my life, I will *still* find happiness. I'll embrace it, and I'll love every second of my life."

That surrendering is no coincidence; it's part of the reason I met my true love not long afterward.

Know your divine worth. Don't settle for just anyone solely for the sake of being in a relationship. So many people will stay in relationships that aren't with the true love of their dreams because they're afraid—afraid to leave, afraid it's too late, afraid they won't find anyone else.

Please know if something doesn't feel right in love, it's not a failure to walk away. That person is not your last option. There are literally billions of people on this planet! I promise you that if a relationship doesn't feel right, there is someone out there more aligned with you.

Don't be afraid to be alone. There is nothing wrong with being single. That's another vital mindset shift to make.

Ask yourself the following questions:

- *Why do I see being single as a bad thing?*
- *What are some empowering things about being single?*
- *How can I enjoy my life exactly as it is right now?*

Oftentimes people think by showing gratitude to the Universe for being single, they'll attract *more* of being single, but it's the opposite. When you show gratitude and appreciation for exactly where you are now and accept where you are now, it raises your vibration. It shows you're not fighting the Universe's plan; you're flowing with it, and *that* vibration is pure magic and will help you get to where you want to be.

Being alone is better than being with the wrong person. Have enough love for yourself to choose *you* over settling for something "okay" just for the sake of having someone.

You don't owe anyone anything. If someone feels off, you don't need to stay with them just because you either think they need you or because you feel bad hurting them. They'll be okay. They'll find their path just as you will find yours. Don't sacrifice your own happiness for the sake of someone else. You'll both find someone more aligned—but neither of you will find true happiness by hanging on to something that isn't working.

The root of heartbreak is often not the loss of a specific person but from losing the idea of what could have been. We mourn the potential of love, but, in truth, who that person was would never match the dream we had in our heads.

The right doors will always open, while the wrong doors will always close. What's meant to be will always be, and the Universe will forever have our backs. If a person leaves your life, or it just doesn't work out, recognize that the Universe is closing this door because it's not your door. It's not for your highest good. Something not working out just means something better is on its way. You can be disappointed, of course. Feel all your feelings, cry, rant, and journal, but deep down, know the Universe has a plan—trust it!

I also see people eager to be in relationships not because they want to be with a specific person but because they want to be with someone, *anyone*. Committing yourself to a relationship should be because you love that person, not because you just want a partner. See the difference.

I'm often baffled by the amount of people who say it's normal to have periods when they can't stand their partners or that their relationships are constantly hard work. Sure, in every partnership, you're not going to be your best self all the time. Disagreements are inevitable; frustrations will pop up. It's most likely not going to be picture-perfect all of the time, but why can't it be good *most* of the time? Why has society set this standard that indoctrinates people to expect love, something that's supposed to be beautiful and magical, to be consistently arduous? Why do we all just accept and settle for this?

Life is cyclical, of course. We're going to have ups and downs. Everything has highs and lows. However, you should be happy, more than not, in love. It's possible to be happy, more than not, in love, yet think of all the ways society blatantly tells us otherwise.

Being with the love of my life has been so incredibly easy. He's my best friend. He was my best friend before there was any romance between us. Sure, we have disagreements from time to time, but they never completely blow up, nor do they last long as we're able to maturely talk and work it out. Working it out has never been impossible either, as we both come from loving, compassionate places. We don't close ourselves off, and we are always respectfully willing to hear each other out and listen to one another's feelings.

Being in a healthy relationship doesn't mean you won't ever argue. It just means when arguments do pop up, you'll hold space for each other to share your thoughts and feelings. You won't be afraid to admit when you're in the wrong and you'll be willing to work together to create a resolution.

Retrain your brain to know that it is possible to have a partner who will rationally talk through disagreements and will work with you to find a solution instead of exploding into a big fight. It's possible to have a partner whom loving is the easiest thing in the world, someone you're grateful for every single day for decades to come.

Marriage and relationships do not have to be the constant "hard work" society tells us they are. They're work, they require effort, but it's the kind of effort you don't mind doing, like working a job you enjoy. You always receive what you believe. I don't know about you, but I always wanted to reject these social narratives. I always believed I'd have a fairy-tale love story, a true love I'd never get sick of, one who'd always hear my side of things (as I would hear his), and a relationship that wasn't hard work but as natural as breathing. I got that because I believed that. That's also what my partner believed before he even met me.

Think of how often you've heard people say that they're happy to be away from their partners or complain about how annoying their partners are. It's so wild that this is an acceptable thing to say. It makes me wonder: *Why are you even together then if you're excited to be apart? Why be in a relationship when it sounds like being single would make you happier?*

Everyone has their own personal preferences within a relationship. Some couples will love to spend all their free time together, others will want more freedom and independence. Just as some couples love sharing the same bed, while others thrive with separate bedrooms or even living separately altogether. There's no right or wrong way. There's someone out there for everyone and it's possible to meet someone who matches your preferences.

However, if you notice someone is *really* excited every time they're away from their partner, it's probably a sign they'd be better off single or with someone else.

Society also has that limiting belief of the "honeymoon stage," when everything is magical and blissful in the beginning. Then once you're out of the honeymoon stage, the romance quickly fades. What's mind-blowing is that people expect this to happen and accept it will happen.

Both my partner and I refuse to believe that love fades, and I know for a fact that is why our love has gotten stronger. We have even more fun now than we did in the beginning. I've seen the same be true for other couples in my life who also refused to give in to that limiting belief about the honeymoon stage.

Love *can* last a lifetime. You can be even more in love 30 years into your relationship than you were one year in. You can definitely find examples of longtime couples in their 60s and beyond who are *still* head over heels in love. Don't let society trick you into believing otherwise. Your mindset is constantly creating everything you experience. Set the intention that every year in your relationship, you fall deeper and deeper in love.

While your belief system is a massive part of staying in love, don't forget to also put in the effort. Once you have love, don't let either of you fall into that trap of thinking that with every passing moment, your relationship is nosediving into the "no longer exciting and romantic" pool. Plan date nights, compliment your partner, flirt, be intimate, surprise them with sweet gifts, and lean into creating magic together. Your mindset will take you far but don't forget you have to take physical action, as well, to support these new beliefs in order to manifest them as your truth. Mindset plus effort is the ultimate formula for success.

Don't doubt your magic! Make your wish for however you want love to be and know it *can* be. It can be that straightforward. Love doesn't have to be a battlefield like people say it is; it can be pure magic.

FAIRY GODMOTHER CONNECTION

The main reason I grew up loving fairy tales was because I absolutely adored the idea of having a fairy godmother. In stories, we often see our main characters at their hardest moments, only to be comforted, saved, and have their deepest wishes granted by their fairy guardians.

Real life can work like this, too!

If we are pure of heart and filled with the best intentions for all involved, our fairies can absolutely help make our greatest wishes come true.

In this exercise, I want you to connect with *your* fairy godmother! As we've seen in countless stories, fairies love granting wishes of romance, so you'll consult with your fairy godmother about your biggest wish for your love life.

Of course, as we've discussed, while working with any elementals, you'll definitely want to make an offering and leave a gift for your fairy godmother as gratitude for her help! These offerings can include treats like chocolate, little golden treasures or charms, or even adding furniture and miniature houses to a fairy garden outside.

Once you've made your offering, sit outside and meditate. If it's during the colder months, feel free to sit inside near plants or flowers. If it's during the warmer months, definitely try this outside in a peaceful spot surrounded by nature.

Scan the QR code to download and listen to the audio version of this meditation found at the back of this book.

Imagine walking through a magical garden. Vibrant flowers, overgrown garden beds, and massive trees surround you. The sunlight sparkles in and out of gaps in the trees' leaves.

The garden feels peaceful. The garden feels safe.

You approach a magical little grove, one that feels extra special to you. Maybe it's filled with your favorite flowers, or fruit trees, or there's an enchanting wooden swing beside a glittering pond. Trust whatever is coming to you.

Twinkling lights bob up and down, surrounding the entire space.

You can feel all the magic surrounding you.

Declare that you will only interact with beings of the highest level of light and love, with the purest intention for all involved.

You feel love radiating through your heart as you make your offering of gratitude.

Present your fairy godmother with a divine gift.

Then, tell your fairy godmother you'd love to meet her, to connect with her, to learn from her.

Wait for her to appear and introduce herself, and take in every aspect of how she is presenting herself to you.

Ask for her name and how long she's been with you.

Then, ask her if it is okay for you to tell her your wish for love. If she says it is, proceed to tell her your heart's deepest desires.

Once you've finished, thank your fairy godmother. She smiles at you and waves her magic wand, surrounding you in a shimmering flurry of glitter.

Notice how you feel. Perhaps you are experiencing a newfound sense of hope, abundance, or excitement. Your fairy godmother tells you your wish has been granted. It's now only a matter of time before it comes true.

Finally, ask your fairy godmother if there is anything you need to do on your end to help make this wish manifest.

Perhaps she'll tell you to keep your heart more open, to believe more, to trust, or that everything is already taken care of. Listen to her advice.

Afterwards, thank her again. Know you can continue to connect with your fairy godmother on a regular basis to help make your wishes come true.

Feel free to take out a journal to write about your experience.

Continue to nurture this relationship like you would any friendship. The more you connect with your fairy godmother and consult with her, the stronger your bond will be.

MEDIA MINDSET

Not only does society have warped views on love, but pop culture and media also affect our beliefs. A lot of fiction shows us that love is messy and complicated, full of tears and breakdowns.

We find ourselves rooting for the couples with the most ups and downs, fights, barriers, and betrayals, thinking these make a relationship more romantic. But that's not true at all. If a relationship is problematic, it's not more romantic; it's just unhealthy.

When I was a teenager, I loved watching all those teen dramas of the 00s. As I got older and reevaluated my mindset around love, I realized those shows had instilled in me the idea that couples who fight, break up and get back together multiple times are the ones to root for, the ones that are more "meant to be."

Because my teenage mind believed that, I attracted an

unhealthy relationship. We broke up and got back together six times over the course of seven months. There was even a love triangle at one point. My 17-year-old self thought all the drama meant we were supposed to be together. Thank the stars, we were not!

Looking back, I realize we were just young and still learning about relationship dynamics. We were figuring out what we each individually wanted in a relationship and what we expected from our partners. Love may be messy sometimes and that's okay, especially if love is new to you and you're figuring out what you want and expect from your relationships. You'll make mistakes; you'll mess up. It's all part of the learning process to help you figure out what you do and don't want in a relationship.

Accept the messes and mistakes but don't confuse drama for romance. Don't glorify problematic couples. True passion is not screaming at each other and then making love like movies tell us it is.

To each their own, of course! All our relationships will look differently, but I'm going to take a wild guess, just by the fact you're reading this book, that you don't want a relationship in which you're always fighting, breaking up, getting back together, and feel like you're dangling on the edge of a precarious cliff.

Love can be whatever you want it to be. Don't let those fictional relationships seep into your subconscious and make you feel like that's what real love is.

You can absolutely watch those shows and movies and read those books! They are super entertaining. I, for one, love a good rom-com drama, and I still adore stories with love triangles, even after surviving one in high school. There's no need to cut off these forms of entertainment just to avoid absorbing their energy. It is, however, important to be cognizant and energetically separate what you're consuming versus what you want to manifest. Recognize that those relationships contain elements that you don't want, and instead, affirm that the opposite is happening for you. As you watch or read, declare to the Universe, "This is just a story; this is not my truth." Then afterward, think about what you *do* want in love.

Gather positive fictional examples of couples who exemplify your romantic desires. This includes couples who love each other beyond words, couples who always listen to each other and are respectful of each other's needs, or couples who are seen as best friends. Absorb the energy of fictional couples who talk their problems out, who are passionate, who grow together, and support each other.

Again, everyone's relationship is different, so everyone's version of their dream romance will vary, but make sure you recognize the good fictional relationships versus the unstable ones and model your own relationship on the good ones.

It can be helpful to feel all the feelings for a positive fictional couple, root for them, and put yourself in their shoes. It's something I did! Remember when I mentioned my romance felt like a real-life version of Jim and Pam from *The Office*? Watching *The* Office and swooning over Jim and Pam helped me embody and feel what a love like that would be like. It absolutely contributed to my rom-com-esque love story manifesting.

The songs we listen to also absolutely have an effect on our love life.

Music seeps into our subconscious mind, so take inventory of the kinds of songs you're absorbing. If they're all about cheating, getting hurt, or being broken, it may just further cement into your brain that that's how love is, thus further manifesting those experiences for you.

Now, just like with shows and books, this doesn't mean should you never listen to these songs again. You can listen to them—especially if they're your favorites! It just means you should be careful of how deeply you feel them, how often you sing them out loud, and just as you would when consuming dramatic media, affirm to the Universe that it is not your truth.

If there's a sad song you love and want to listen to, do it, but maybe listen to a few uplifting love songs afterward.

Then, make some empowering love affirmations about what you do wish to experience. Say the following affirmations: "Everything always works out in my love life! I'm so happy and in love. I'm blessed to have a healthy, stable, loving relationship." These affirmations amplify positive love energy and keep retraining your mind to expect that love is blissful.

My recommendation is to make an empowering love playlist. Create a compilation of all the happiest and most romantic love songs you can think of, ones that empower you and set the stage for the type of relationship you want to experience.

Whenever you feel like it (or whenever you particularly need it), listen to this playlist and *feel* the messages of the songs. Envision your perfect romance as you listen to your playlist. Doing this on a regular basis is an amazingly easy and powerful way to call in your true love. For an extra boost, you can also combine this principle with candle magic, which is your next exercise.

CANDLE SPELL FOR PASSIONATE LOVE

It's time to light the flame of romance! Candles have long been used as magical tools to help beautiful souls energetically attract more of what they want. Candles also happen to be a strong symbol of a romantic night in, so what better tool to use to manifest your dream romance?

For this exercise, get a brand new, unused candle. The candle can be white to call in pure love, pink for playful love, or red for passionate love. When I did this exercise many years ago, I sourced an amazing rose quartz candle. It smelled of roses and had rose quartz (the crystal of love) fixed atop. Having that crystal energy infused into the candle not only gave the spell an extra boost but also helped me believe more. That's the point in all of this: to set yourself up to believe, feel, and *know* it's all possible for you!

Now, before you light the candle, set the mood for romance in the rest of your room. Turn down the lights, and wear something romantic, that you'd wear on your dream date night. Spray perfume or diffuse essential oils, and, of course, play romantic music.

Pick one love song that represents the exact type of love you wish to experience. I recommend listening to the lyrics thoroughly before starting the ritual, just to make sure every part of the song feels aligned. A lot of seemingly beautiful love songs have some underlying unhealthy messages, and we don't want that! Choose a love song that represents healthy love, strong love, loyal love, and one that is full of passionate romance. It's also important to make sure this love song is not associated with anyone else in your mind. It may be your favorite love song, but if you associate it with your ex or you used to listen to it while daydreaming about an unrequited crush, it won't do. Don't even use a song that was featured in your favorite film, as you may associate it with the fictional couple. This song needs to be fresh and free of any attachments. Trust your intuition; you'll know when you've found the right song.

For extra magical energy, similar to my rose quartz candle, make a crystal grid around your candle. Surround your candle on all sides (north, south, east, and west) with crystals that invoke romance. I particularly recommend you include rose quartz for divine love, carnelian for passion, and clear quartz for clear intentions. Then, it's up to you which other crystals you add.

Personalize it! Go to your local crystal shop and trust your intuition. Ask your fairies to guide you toward the crystals that would be best in your grid. Manifestation is personal to each of us, so we should always allow our intuition to lead the way.

Here are some of my favorite love crystals to help you get started

Crystal	**Purpose**
Rose Quartz	Divine love
Carnelian	Passion
Clear Quartz	Clear intentions
Citrine	Happiness and manifesting
Malachite	Opens heart chakra and manifesting
Pyrite	Abundance of love
Sardonyx	Luck in love
Unicorn Stone	Joy and fairy-tale romance
Selenite	Clear energy
Fire & Ice Quartz	Clear intentions and manifesting
Sunstone	Joy
Black Tourmaline	Protection against negativity in relationships

Once you have your song and crystals and set the mood, it's time to begin!

Light your candle, and as you do, thank the salamanders, the fire fairies, for being with you, for guiding this flame, and for helping to ignite your heart with passion. Make them an offering, maybe by adding a carnelian crystal specifically noted to be for them.

Listen to the full duration of the song. I recommend putting it on repeat a couple of times. Doing this ritual for 11 minutes will help you align with that manifesting energy, as 11 is a master number that represents dreams manifesting (like how you always make a wish at 11:11). As you listen, start to visualize and feel deep within your heart exactly how you'd feel if your true love was with you *now.* Get excited. Celebrate! Feel your true love's embrace; feel their love; visualize going on romantic dates; see yourself getting married if you so wish. The more you feel it in your heart, the more the Universe will match that energy and bring it to you.

After visualizing, spend a moment writing down all the qualities you wish your dream partner to have. Fold your list up and put it underneath your candle in the center of your grid to allow it to charge.

Repeat "thank you" several times, and know in your heart that true love is already on its way. When you're done, snuff out the candle (don't blow it out; otherwise, you will blow out the spell), and visualize, perhaps in a flourishing cinematic font, "*To be continued...*"

Do this ritual every single night (try not to skip a night!) until the candle has fully burned through. Tell yourself that every time you do it, you are a day closer to your true love.

The candle spell is complete on the night your candle has fully burned, and your wish will be granted within a few weeks. *However*, your wish might not always appear in the way you expect.

When I did this ritual for myself, I didn't realize I had *already* met my true love. He was currently my best friend, but I refused to acknowledge my romantic feelings for him. I did this candle ritual, and within two weeks to the day of finishing the candle, I went to that Christmas party I mentioned earlier, where at the end of the night, one of my friend's co-workers asked me out on a date. I was so excited that the candle ritual worked; it actually brought me romance! However, you already know what happened: when I went on the date, I realized I didn't want to be there with this guy or anyone else; I wanted to be with my best friend. I *finally* admitted to myself that I was in love with *him*!

(Please don't feel bad for my date that fateful night; he wound up finding his true love not long after, too!)

This ritual *will* bring you love. However, as my experience shows, it may awaken you to newfound clarity of who it really is you love. It could bring you a romance that may not be the one, but a person who will make you realize an important lesson about yourself in love, a lesson that is vital for you to learn before meeting the one. It may also bring you someone who will lead you to the one, or it could very directly bring you the one. Be open to all the possibilities, and know when you do this, you *will* receive whatever you *need* in love. Trust the Universe has a plan in place and a reason for everything.

WELCOME ALL POSSIBILITIES

While refining your thoughts, speaking your love into existence, and shunning limiting beliefs, another incredible way to manifest love is to celebrate other couples!

When I first started dating my now husband, most of my friends were happy for me, but one of my best friends was particularly excited. She'd hype us up, tell us how cute we were, and was genuinely delighted by our love. Because she celebrated my love story, I think it's no coincidence that she also met someone *at work*, which developed into the same kind of friends-to-lovers, silly, fun, playful romantic relationship.

Oftentimes, when people are single and see other couples, there's a knee-jerk reaction to roll their eyes, feel mad, or pity themselves. Seeing a couple laughing and holding hands makes them realize what they don't have. Seeing engagement posts reminds them it's not happening for them. While all these feelings are valid, understand it's not the Universe pouring salt in the wound. In fact, it's the opposite.

If you're seeing loving couples that means it's on your energetic frequency. You only ever see things you are an energetic match for, so if you see engagements, weddings, anniversaries, and happy couples, the Universe is saying you are currently on the frequency of love. This means it's time to celebrate!

Shift your sadness to excitement that the Universe is showing you what's possible for you and that with each day that passes, you're getting closer and closer to experiencing it for yourself. Celebrate those couples as if you are celebrating yourself. Be genuinely happy for them, and send them good wishes and blessings.

Your subconscious brain doesn't recognize if you're saying things (bad or good) about someone else; it takes everything you say or think as directed toward you, yourself, personally. So if you're celebrating another couple's engagement, your brain will absorb those joyful feelings and energetically project that to the Universe. The Universe will rearrange things to set the stage to manifest an engagement for you.

From here on out, every time you see another couple, release all feelings of envy and instead celebrate them. See them as direct confirmation that you're on the right frequency to manifest love.

Open your eyes to the possibility that you can find love anywhere!

Another common limiting belief I've found among friends and clients is that they want to meet someone in real life, but genuinely believe the apps are their only option. While there's nothing wrong with the apps, and they are great tools that have helped a lot of love stories blossom, just remember, if you think that they are your only option, if that's your story, the Universe is going to match that frequency. Thus, the apps will be your only place to meet a partner.

Shift your focus and start to notice all the potential ways you could meet someone. There could be a new hire at your job; you could meet them at the gym; or you could bump into them at the grocery store as you're both reaching for the same sweet potato. They could be your server, or bartender, or deliver a package to your home. They could be waiting in line behind you at the ATM, sitting next to you at a hockey game, or just one towel over at the beach. They could be at a friend of a friend's birthday party. They could be sitting next to you in a doctor's waiting room, jogging ahead of you at the park, or enrolling in the same meditation class. You could meet them while repairing a flat tire or at a comic convention. You just never know!

Expand your horizons and realize they could be *anywhere*. Recognize and accept the possibility that you can meet anyone, anywhere, at any time—and the Universe will match this frequency. I bet you'll start to notice a lot more attractive potential partners when you're out and about living your life. Celebrate this, and see it as a sign that your life is abundant with potential love!

To enhance this aligned action say "yes" to more social events. It's hard to meet someone in real life sitting on your couch, so get yourself out there! Join clubs or take adult classes for things you are interested in. You never know who might also be attending. Even if you don't meet the love of your life, I'm sure you'll make new friends with similar interests, and you never know who those new friends might know. So many people get introduced to their true love through someone else.

If you find someone cute and nice while out, don't be afraid to initiate conversation and even flirt. It's perfectly okay if you're shy. However, if you're trying to find love, it's good to be a slightly bolder version of yourself, put yourself out there, and open your heart to give things a chance.

But don't change yourself! You want to be 100% you because that's exactly who the love of your life will fall in love with. Step into the most confident version of yourself, and don't be afraid to interact with people you're interested in out of fear of rejection; for all you know, you may not even like them. You have nothing to lose, but you'll never know if you don't try. Don't let the fear of rejection stop you. Everyone gets rejected; everyone gets heartbroken at one point or another. You're not alone.

If you're hurting, give yourself proper time to heal, feel everything you need to, and know that there is no timetable for healing a broken heart. Your feelings are always valid; honor them. Just know that someday, it won't hurt so much anymore. Someday, things will feel better—you'll barely think about the person who hurt you. Someday, you'll find someone who loves you unconditionally and is aligned with everything you've ever wanted. Someday, you'll see why things happened as they did and feel grateful that it didn't work out with anyone else.

Sometimes, we want something to work out so badly that we neglect to see the red flags and warning signs. If someone feels sketchy, they probably are—deeply trust your instincts here; they're always right. That's why you are connecting with your angels, fairies, and mermaids. The more consistently you practice tuning into your intuition, the stronger it'll get, and it'll be easier for you to recognize and trust your instincts.

Keep in mind classic excuses like "It's not you; it's me," or "I like you, but I'm not looking for a relationship right now," specifically said after going out on a date, clearly looking to start a relationship, are almost always just that—*excuses*. If the absolute love of that person's life walked in and completely wowed them, do you really think they would say, "I'm just not looking for a relationship right now" after their date? No! They would find a way to make it work despite whatever is going on in their lives.

Sure, there are always exceptions and maybe this person isn't making up an excuse. Maybe the timing is off. Maybe they're self-sabotaging. Maybe they genuinely wanted to try but their mental health is struggling. Maybe something difficult is going on in their lives. Use your discernment. You can even ask the angels, fairies, and mermaids to help make this person's intentions clear. More often than not though, people aren't going to deny themselves happiness or true love. If they genuinely like you and are mentally and emotionally stable, they will find a way to make it work.

You deserve someone who is all in on you. Don't put up with someone's excuses. See them for exactly what they are and know you deserve better than that. You deserve to be someone's first choice; you deserve someone genuinely excited to start something with *you*, who is fascinated by *you*, who wants to know all about *you*, who wants to have fun with you, and who enriches your life experience. You deserve someone who sees the complete gem you are and can barely believe how lucky they are to have met you. You should feel all of that about them, too. You should be excited about a future with them—not just excited about romance in general, but excited about *this* romance with *them* specifically.

If someone seriously likes you, they will put in the effort without question. They will text you back; they will go out of their way to see you. They won't play games or ignore you to seem cool. They won't be afraid to show you how much they like you.

Never settle for just okay in love. Love is one area where you don't want to compromise. You deserve and are worthy of someone's full effort and attention.

Recognize the signs of harmful relationships versus healthy ones. Your partner should never control you, make you feel bad, or put you down. They should always be a support system, uplifting and encouraging. Even if you don't agree on certain topics or interests, you should mutually respect each other's opinions, likes, and dislikes. They should respect your life choices and your boundaries—and vice versa. You want to be aligned, especially regarding ideals and values and what you want your future and dream life to be.

Don't be afraid to step away from what no longer serves you. If you finally manifested love, and it's not what you want, don't feel like you're being ungrateful. It's like being hungry at a restaurant and when your meal finally comes, it's not what you ordered. Maybe you even try a bite, but you don't like the taste. Are you going to settle for something you don't like or go hungry? No, you send it back and ask for what you ordered.

The Universe will not be offended if you reject someone you manifested into your life. In fact, it will be proud of you for saying no (it knows that person wasn't your true love, too!). Don't be afraid to say "no". No one is ever your last option! When one person leaves, it just creates space for another.

Above all, take pressure off yourself when dating and know

that not every person you meet will be the love of your life. I used to get extreme anxiety before dates. To calm myself down, I'd remind myself that either this person *is* the love of my life, in which case everything will work out, so why worry? Or they're *not* the love of my life, in which case their opinion of me doesn't matter. One day, this situation will be long forgotten, and I *will* be happily in love with the right person.

KISSING FROGS AND LEAPING FORWARD

In high school, my friend's mom would tell us, "You have to kiss a few frogs," which means you'll date some not-so-great people before you find the one. That's normal; everyone experiences that. Don't let bad dates or bad people discourage you. Don't give them any power over you. Don't allow them to scar you and close your heart off. Their opinion of you means nothing and does not diminish your value whatsoever.

Another great thing to keep in mind when experiencing rejection—notice I didn't say *if* because it really is part of the journey—it's protection. If a date doesn't work out, it's the Universe intervening because that person is not right for you. Trust the process; if things end, it's because a new beginning is just around the corner. Whether you decide someone isn't right for you or your date initiates the ending, rejection is always protection and redirection away from who's not right and toward who is.

Sometimes relationships end only to reconnect months, years, or even decades later. Sometimes it is just about timing and it winds up working out better down the line. Sometimes both parties need to learn a lesson before they are ready for each other. Trust that what's meant to be will always find a way. If a relationship doesn't immediately work out, you never know what the future holds. If you are genuinely meant to be together, nothing can stop it.

Ancient Chinese culture shares the idea of the invisible red string. This theory always made me feel better and reminds me of my favorite Taylor Swift song, "Invisible String." The story goes that at birth, two soulmates are tied together by an invisible red string, and no matter how much the string stretches or tangles, it will never sever, and they'll always find their way to each other. The string will yank you away from who's not meant for you and draw you closer and closer to who is. You can't mess it up. Whatever path you go down, you're always destined to meet someday in some way. Even if things don't work out the first time, you'll always find your way back to each other.

Nothing can happen before the Universe is ready for it. Everything unfolds in true divine timing. Divine timing is like baking a cake. You wouldn't take your cake out of the oven after only a few minutes of baking. It'd be soupy and likely give you a stomachache if you tried to eat it. But if you wait the full duration and have patience until it's cooled and decorated, it will be the most stunning, delicious cake and well worth the wait.

Love is the same. Sometimes, our soulmates don't show up right away because we have life lessons we need to learn without them, or they have lessons they need to experience before us. Perhaps your true love lives somewhere else and needs to decide to move closer to you; maybe they need to leave their job and get hired at a new one (where you work!).

You'd also want you and your true love to be in the right state of mind, single, and emotionally available to date and fall in love. It'd be devastating to meet them while they were still in a relationship with someone else, so maybe the delay is they need to step away from a relationship that is no longer aligned so they (and their current partner) can find true happiness.

There are so many moving parts; you just never know what's happening behind the scenes. Embody patience! Time moves so quickly. Honestly, think of a moment in the past when you *really* wanted something that seemingly took forever. Maybe it was getting your driver's license, visiting your dream destination, or for your favorite author to publish the next installment in their book series. How long ago was that? Months? Years? It's something that seemingly took forever but is well in the past already now.

Someday, you'll be happy with the love of your life and realize you've known them for a year, then 5 years, 10 years, and many more.

With my own love story, my younger self felt like it was taking forever to meet my husband. Now, I look back and recognize how long he's already been in my life. If we had met earlier, the timing might not have been right. We are 3 years apart, so if we'd met in high school or college, when I was a freshman and he was a senior, at that young age I would have been intimidated by an older guy. Once we were out of school, we were both dating other people. It wouldn't have worked to meet while seeing someone else. Those other people taught us invaluable lessons but ultimately weren't right for us. We both needed to remove those people from our lives, heal heartbreaks, and align our energy to be open to receive the true love we both knew we always deserved.

I was also single for several years, which led me to dive deeper into manifestation, specifically around love, to master the energy and mindset of love. During that time, I healed my heart and learned how to help my friends, clients, and now you with this book. I'm *grateful* for that time because I discovered what was necessary for my soul's path and life purpose.

In hindsight, I can clearly see that my husband and I met at the most opportune moment for both of us. We were both single, healed, and met in an environment that allowed us to become friends before slowly falling in love. We got to know each other on a purely platonic level, which gave us a stable foundation. I also got to experience developing a crush on him, wondering if he felt the same, which, in its own way, is pretty romantic. I love how my love story unfolded; it's better than I imagined.

It's funny remembering how frustrated I once was, but now I can see how it all happened in the best way at the best time.

One day, I promise you, you'll feel the same. While your love story may seem like it's taking longer than you'd like, trust the timing. Someday, it'll feel like it took no time at all.

FINDING LOVE WITH ARCHANGEL CHAMUEL

Archangel Chamuel is amazing at helping us find love. Chamuel has a romantic light pink and soft blue aura, and along with Jophiel and Michael, is considered one of the romance angels. With Cupid-like vibes, Chamuel is happy to connect soulmates and will lead you down the path to meet yours—all in divine timing, of course.

In this meditation, you'll connect with Archangel Chamuel to tell them what you want and to allow them to use their magic to lead you to your true love.

While you can ask Chamuel for guidance, understand they will only share what you need to know in the present moment. Angels are the ultimate teachers; they love to help but they also love to let us learn. They recognize the need for us to exercise our free will, make our own decisions, and experience life (all the ups and downs of it) rather than just take a shortcut to our happily ever afters. Angelic guidance will always be exactly what our souls need to hear at the time of asking.

With that, keep your heart open and be ready to receive whatever it is you need right now.

Scan the QR code to download and listen to the audio version of this meditation found at the back of this book.

Take a deep breath in and a deep breath out.

Take a deep breath in and a deep breath out.

Imagine beautiful white light coming down from the divine, filling up your crown chakra, connecting you to divinity, and surrounding you in a beautiful bubble of light.

The white light shimmers and transforms into beautiful shades of pink and blue.

A magical daytime sky surrounds you, encasing you in pure magic, encasing you in love.

You feel a sparkling, protective energy surrounding you. You feel the energy of love and romance. You feel the magic of Archangel Chamuel with you.

Call upon Chamuel and ask them to be with you. Thank them for their help. Send them lots of love and gratitude.

Now, Chamuel hands you a quill pen and a golden scroll. Chamuel requests you write down everything you wish to receive in love.

You take the pen and scroll, and you begin to write. Describe in detail all the emotions you'd like to feel and all the qualities you'd love your partner to have.

When you've finished, offer your list to Chamuel. Chamuel holds your list to their heart. You watch as your list grows brighter and brighter, until it disappears completely, and is absorbed into the divine.

Chamuel smiles at you, assuring you your wishes have been heard and it will all happen in divine timing.

Next, ask Archangel Chamuel for details or clues about your true love soulmate. Ask if they can share what kind of person your true love is. Ask if there are any places you need to go or any mindset shifts you need to make.

Tune into your intuition and allow the conversation with Chamuel to continue for as long as you need.

When you feel the conversation is complete, thank Archangel Chamuel for all their guidance, and know you can call upon them again whenever you wish.

Feel free to journal about your experience connecting with Archangel Chamuel.

You can continue to work with Archangel Chamuel by simply asking them to lead you and the love of your life to each other. Ask Chamuel to help you both take all the correct steps to cross paths when the timing is right and to have a long-lasting, healthy relationship filled with harmony and true bliss.

SEE THE POSITIVES

If you have a bad date or a romance that doesn't work out, another great mindset shift is to twist it into a positive. Celebrate the fact that you did technically attract a date; you attracted someone you were interested in who was also interested in you romantically. See it as proof it's possible for you. If you met someone to date this time, you can do it again, and next time, the person will be a step up and even more aligned. Show the Universe that you are grateful it brought potential love to you.

You know that feeling when you give someone a gift, and their reaction is pure joy and gratitude—it makes you want to keep giving, whether it's for birthdays, holidays, or just because. On the flip side, when someone reacts with indifference or rudeness, it naturally discourages you from wanting to give again. The Universe has kind of the same vibe. When you show deep appreciation for everything in your path and gratitude for attracting love in some form, the Universe will want to give you bigger and better. If you're bitter and unappreciative, the Universe doesn't vibe with that. You slip into that lack mindset and block yourself from receiving more unexpected gifts.

Appreciate everything and see value and beauty even in the things that didn't work out because they're all either lessons to help you on your path to love or tantalizing glimpses of what could be possible for you.

Contrary to popular belief, dating is supposed to be fun. What's the whole point of dating? To enjoy yourself, have a nice evening, flirt, feel cute, and experience romance—don't turn it into an arduous chore.

A great affirmation is, "I always have fun on dates. I attract amazing experiences and lovely people." Create your new story as someone who always has fun on dates, always finds a way to meet people, has plenty of options, meets high-quality people, and genuinely enjoys dating.

ROSE PETAL RITUAL

Roses are the ultimate symbol of passionate love for a reason. Like a rose quartz crystal, they hold the vibration of romance and will bring it wherever they bloom. Flower fairies are part of the reason beautiful gardens are possible, and in this exercise, we are going to work with the flower fairies to make a magical love potion.

Gather organic roses that aren't sprayed with pesticides or chemicals and remove the petals. If you gather roses straight from nature or your own garden, thank the flower fairies and, as you already know, leave them a little gift in exchange (or plant even more flowers for them!).

As there are many different colors of roses and each has a different meaning, you can connect with and ask the flower fairies to guide you on which color would be best for you. Pick whichever color the flower fairies advise or whichever ones you feel most drawn to. You can also use more than one color if guided to do so.

Petal Colour	**Purpose**
Red	Calls in a passionate romance
Pink	Attracts a light-hearted, fun romance
White	Invites a romance with pure intentions
Yellow	Brings happiness and mutual trust in love

Wash your rose petals with water and put them in a cooking pot. Add enough water to completely cover the petals (purified, natural water would be best). Set your stovetop burner on low heat, cover the pot with a lid, and let your potion simmer until the rose petals have lost their color (about 30–45 minutes).

As the pot simmers, stir your petals in six circles clockwise (in numerology, six is the number for romance), and as you do, feel love and gratitude.

Whisper into the pot words that reflect the type of love you'd like to experience in your dream romance, such as *happily ever after, passion, loyalty, fun, laughter, magical, dreamy, commitment, true love*. Know that those words will be absorbed into your rose water.

After infusing the brew with your words, stir the petals around six more times, clockwise.

Finally, place your hands to your heart and repeat "thank you" six times, and then place your hands over your simmering rose water and repeat "thank you" six more times as you send all your heart's desires into your potion.

Once the pot has finished simmering and the petals have all lost their color, let it cool completely, then pour your potion into an empty perfume spray bottle.

Feel free to add mini rose quartz chips to the bottom of the spray bottle.

Now you've made a magical rose water love potion, set with your intentions. Spray yourself with your potion as often as you'd like, knowing every time you do so, you become a magnet for love.

AFFIRMING LOVE

One day, you'll wake up next to the love of your life, having been with them for many years. You'll smile at each other, they'll kiss your forehead, and then you'll get up and have breakfast together. All will be well.

You deserve it, and it's possible for you! You deserve the best. You deserve the most amazing version of your love story, in whatever way that looks like to you.

Your mind is your most powerful tool. Whatever you feed into it will manifest for you. Reclaim your magic. Believe love can happen at any time for you. For all you know, you could meet the love of your life next year, next week, or even tomorrow!

Celebrate other couples and recognize they are proof of what's possible for you.

Speak generous uplifting words; think appreciative empowering thoughts. Where you allow your energy to dwell is absolutely what's going to manifest.

Love Affirmations

These affirmations are for you to repeat and write as often as possible. Deeply feel them as you write or speak them:

I am loved; I am in love; I am love.

I am so happily in love with the most amazing soul.

I am so grateful for my partner. They respect me, trust me, and bring me joy.

It is possible for me to have lifelong true love.

I am a magnet for romantic love.

I embody the version of myself who is happily in a relationship with the love of my life.

Self-Love

Have you ever daydreamed about being a completely different person? Not someone specific, just a vague other human with a profession you think is super cool, looks a certain way, has certain life experiences, and grew up in a different part of the world?

Did you know that before you chose to incarnate onto Earth you mapped out much of your life? As I mentioned earlier, human free will is very much a thing. Our life is our own to create. Our environment and experiences mold us into the person we are. We choose our paths and learn to adapt to the unplanned ups and downs. However, throughout my studies connecting with Spirit, I've learned that before we incarnate, our soul chooses certain checkpoints to hit in life. We come in with the intention of lessons we need to learn, the people we will interact with, our interests and natural abilities, who our parents or guardians are, where we grow up, our ethnicity, and what we look like.

Let that sink in. In the same way that you may daydream now

about being someone else, your soul once daydreamed about being *you*.

It seriously had every option in the world of who to be and chose you. It chose you over all the types of people you currently think are better or wish you could be. It's only fair to honor your soul's choice. Honor that dream, and start to see what your soul saw in you. Your soul saw something marvelous about being born where you were, looking the way you do, having your talents, and your personality. This is who you wanted to be.

Part of manifesting love stems from embodying love itself. Like energy always attracts like, so how can we attract love if we don't radiate love within? It may seem like a cliché, but it's entirely true. In order to vibrate at the frequency to receive love, you must feel love for all that you are, have been, and will be.

You are the only person you are ever going to be with 24/7 for the rest of your life. Instead of constantly fighting with yourself or tearing yourself down, make peace with yourself and learn to see all the beauty your soul saw when it created this amazing human to be for an entire lifetime.

As we've discussed, everything is energy, including all the beautiful cells that make up your body. Every part of you works so hard to keep you alive, and your cells are constantly responding to the energy of you. They're constantly tuned in and listening to everything you say and everything you think.

When you spend energy speaking and thinking negative things about yourself, complaining about who you are, and putting yourself down, you are lowering the vibration of the energy that surrounds you and exists within you. Not only can other people feel that in your aura, whether they consciously realize it or not, but you wind up manifesting your words as your truth.

Years ago, when I first took my intuition development classes, the majority of the women taking the class alongside me were about 20 years older than I was. One day, we talked about the power of the words you speak about yourself. They all chimed in and told tales about how, when they were my age, they would complain constantly about their weight and appearance. Now, they look back at pictures of themselves and realize they were so beautiful, despite not seeing it then. But now, in their 40s and beyond, they still felt unhappy with themselves. They felt the untrue words and complaints they used to speak about themselves manifested in their reality. I disagreed with them because their 40-something selves all looked beautiful to me no matter what size or how many wrinkles they thought they had, but this principle of our words manifesting stuck with me. It reminded me to be kind to myself.

From then on, I made a conscious effort to try to stop saying anything negative about myself. I would look in the mirror and tell myself I looked great and affirm that with every year that passes, I would grow more beautiful because aging is a gift. By removing the word "ugly" from my vocabulary, I've grown more confident in the way I look. I feel way more comfortable in my 30s without make-up than I ever did in my 20s.

Do I still have negative thoughts about myself from time to

time? Of course. We're human. These thoughts are going to pop up. The key is not to let the negative self-talk win and overpower you. When I notice negative self-talk, I take a few deep breaths, imagine letting the words go, and then find something nice to say about myself. Even if you can only find one thing, like the color of your eyes or the cute freckles on your nose or the bounciness of your curls, it will help start to retrain your brain to recognize more of the good.

The same goes for weight. While I firmly believe every size is beautiful, we want to be where we each feel comfortable. In my early 20s, my weight was slightly higher than I felt comfortable with, and then in my early 30s, after losing my mom several months before my wedding, I struggled with my weight being lower than I felt comfortable with. However, anytime I'd find myself criticizing my body, I'd stop myself and send thanks to my body for all it does to keep me alive. I'd appreciate the vessel that houses my soul and I'd tell myself I was beautiful no matter what size because I was me.

Similarly, in my early 20s and teens, I struggled with acne. None of the topical creams I'd try would give me the lasting clear skin I desired. So, I took to manifesting. Not only would I affirm my skin was clear, but I'd also tell myself I was beautiful even with acne. I'd send gratitude to my skin every single time I looked in the mirror. I think it's no coincidence, that after months of consistently appreciating my skin, the acne finally cleared up.

Whenever I focused more on appreciating myself, the more I nourished and cared for myself properly, it helped me feel more comfortable within my body.

Your body is always responding

to you and your words. Be mindful.

If you look in the mirror and think about how unhappy you are with your body, or if you make self-deprecating jokes about how clumsy or forgetful you are, or you complain about the condition of your skin, your body will pick up on that. The energy of your body listens to you. Your cells listen to you. Your entire being absorbs everything you say, and, if you are unkind to yourself, it will manifest and cement the very things you *don't* want.

This is good news! This means if you can look in the mirror, compliment yourself, and affirm you are beautiful enough, talented enough, smart enough, and capable enough—your cells will listen to *that.* Your energy will absorb *that*, and those positive aspects will manifest as your truth.

How many times have you looked in the mirror and felt happy with your appearance, only to go about your day and receive a wave of compliments? You believed you were attractive so that radiated within every cell of your body, and *that* became your truth. And *other* people felt that energy from you, too!

Don't forget to also appreciate all the less tangible qualities that make you beautiful. Acknowledge what a good friend you are or how kind you are to animals. Maybe you bake the best chocolate chip cookies or you're absolutely hilarious and light up every room you're in.

It's time to upgrade your self-talk. Going forward, please speak kind words and think compassionate thoughts about yourself because they are everything. You are not only constantly manifesting your reality, you are manifesting yourself.

SELF-LOVE AFFIRMATIONS

Archangel Jophiel is my favorite angel to work with for self-love. She's the angel of beauty whose purpose is to help us feel good about ourselves inside and out.

Whether you need a big boost of confidence or just want to look pretty for an event, Jophiel is your angel! It's not too trivial to ask her to help you have a good hair day. I 100% asked her for assistance on my wedding day. Jophiel is happy to help!

She *wants* you to look and feel your best because when you feel beautiful, you raise your vibration. When you raise your vibration, it ripples out and raises the collective vibration; the whole planet benefits from that good energy.

When you start seeing the beauty in yourself, you start to notice it more in every area of your life. The more you feel love for everything you are now, the more you become a magnet attracting love into your life—love *for* living your current life and attracting the future love *of* your life.

It's also great to work with Jophiel to create beauty affirmations, such as:

- *I am beautiful inside and out, just by being me.*

- *I shine brightly as me.*
- *I love and appreciate all that I am.*
- *I see myself as the radiant, stunning soul I am.*

Using these affirmations throughout your day will absolutely boost your frequency. Over time, it will help your subconscious mind accept it as your truth.

If you don't currently feel comfortable saying, "I am beautiful," it's okay. Ease yourself into it by adding "I am choosing to believe" before the affirmations:

- *I am choosing to believe I am beautiful.*
- *I am choosing to believe I am worthy.*
- *I am choosing to believe I am incredible.*

Phrasing them this way helps prevent resistance in your body and any mental pushback against the affirmation. By gently starting with "I am choosing to believe," you'll gradually reach a point where you feel comfortable affirming,

> *"I am beautiful. I am worthy. I am incredible."*

Don't underestimate the power of beauty affirmations. While you are beautiful at all stages of life, the more you speak into existence that *you* feel good about yourself, inside and out, the more you'll radiate that aura of love.

ARCHANGEL JOPHIEL MORNING BEAUTY ROUTINE

In the morning, before you start getting ready, ask Archangel Jophiel to be with you. Imagine a glowing pink light descending around you from the divine, surrounding you and encompassing your entire aura. Thank her for her presence and love.

Then, ask for her help to see all the beauty within you.

Look into the mirror and *really* look at yourself. Don't shy away. List five things you love about your appearance, such as your pretty eyes or how cute your curvy thighs look in skirts. Then, list five things you love about who you are as a person, like how you're kind, thoughtful, or fantastic at recalling 90s pop culture trivia.

Change it up. Don't say the same things every single day; actively find new things to recognize and appreciate about yourself. If you feel stuck, ask Jophiel to pop an idea of what you can love about yourself into your head.

After you've made your lists, call upon Jophiel to guide you toward an aligned outfit that feels good for your energy that day. Go to your closet and see where you feel led. Honestly, asking Jophiel for help choosing my outfit has been such a timesaver! I call upon her guidance and trust whatever jumps out at me. Sometimes, it'll feel like a certain outfit has glowing energy; other times, the exact outfit idea might pop into my head, or I might even feel pulled to try a combination I've never done before. Be open to all possibilities and whatever way this intuitive guidance shows up for you.

As you're getting dressed, ask Jophiel to help you feel comfortable in your body, bestow a great hair day, and assist with lovely make-up (if you choose to wear make-up).

As you continue to get ready and dressed, repeat your favorite self-love affirmations. You can also ask Archangel Jophiel for fresh insights and uplifting words to help you recognize your amazing qualities and boost your confidence.

Jophiel guides us not only to experience the beauty within us but to see the beauty in our lives as a whole. Take a few moments to think about everything you adore about your life. Feel gratitude toward the people, places, and things that make you smile.

Appreciate things beyond your personal sphere, too, like the magic of sunsets, the whimsical beauty of butterflies, and the majesty of rainbows. Appreciate generosity between strangers, romantic kisses in the rain, the cuteness of baby animals. Open your eyes to the beauty that is the human experience.

As you commute to work or run errands or go about your day, continue to feel the presence of Archangel Jophiel and actively notice all the things that make life great. Feel gratitude for it all.

One major thing that can block us from manifesting love is feeling like we don't have love in our lives at all. Love is more than just romance. Love is friendship; love is family; love is a really good book; love is a compelling TV series; love is chocolate ice cream; love is a flower garden; love is summer; love is whatever makes your heart sing.

Allow Jophiel to open your eyes every single day to the fact that love is all around you! You have *so* much love in your life already. Notice and appreciate it—because where our attention goes, energy flows, and our manifestations grow!

Regularly hyping yourself up to all the love within you and all the love that surrounds you will make you a magnet for even more love, including the romance you've been dreaming of!

HIGH-VIBE SOCIAL MEDIA

You are what you attract. You are what you give attention to. You are what you normalize. If, like in the above exercise, you normalize self-love, self-love becomes your norm. But, if you normalize self-loathing and self-depreciation, that becomes your norm.

One of the biggest problems in the self-love department has come from the internet. Social media has normalized disliking yourself, and people have gotten into the habit of making fun of themselves just for likes and shares. Sure, we definitely all can learn to laugh at ourselves once in a while, but when you are constantly scrolling through or posting jokes about being "human trash," about being anxious and tired all the time, or complaining about how bad life is—your energy will start to believe that.

Don't feed your mindset with that part of the internet. Just because it's a truth others have accepted doesn't mean it has to be yours. If you see these kinds of self-deprecating internet posts, just send love from the Universe to whoever posted it. Affirm that the opposite is true for you. Feel love and gratitude for everything you are and all the magic that life offers. If you create these kinds of self-deprecating posts, I recommend pressing pause on that and seeing how your life shifts.

Another issue with social media and self-love is the constant need to compare ourselves to others. Again, remember your soul chose to be you, *not someone else,* for a reason!

If you're feeling envious of another person or lifestyle, keep in mind that we only ever see what's on our energetic frequency. The fact that you're seeing someone else have what you want means it's possible for you, too. If you see someone with all the self-confidence you wish you had or the relationship you wish you had, remember it's the Universe showing you it's possible for you, too. As you scroll past, instead of allowing the lives of others on the internet to make you feel bad, compliment them. Comment if you feel inclined, or just state it in your head. Then, pay *yourself* a compliment. This will add to your vibration of good energy and self-love.

Unfollow or mute accounts whose vibe brings you down, and instead, choose to follow uplifting accounts. Follow people who post inspiring words or daily encouragement. Follow more accounts that post things you love, like cute ducklings falling asleep on flowers or people who sample the best cupcakes in town.

Social media can be used to either lower or raise your vibration; it's just about cultivating the content you consume and the content you share. The content you put out is also tied to your vibration and affects the vibration of others. Be mindful about what posts you re-share. Share more uplifting words, inspirational guidance, or things that make you smile. Re-share laughs. Re-share kindness. Re-share hope. Use social media as a tool for good to promote awareness, to help those in need within your community or even globally. Comment kind words on your friends' posts or even comment kind words on a stranger's posts—you never know, it may just make their day!

BELIEFS AND IDENTITY TO NOURISH SELF-LOVE

We can spend a lifetime defining ourselves based on what others have told us about who we are. Especially in our formative years, we let these opinions shape our sense of identity. Our internal identity is a compilation of all the opinions, comments, compliments, reactions, and judgements we have received. Some of this conditioning is positive and some of it will be negative.

Our ability to love ourselves is deeply connected to how we see ourselves. By exploring, healing, and reframing our identity, we can create major shifts in boosting that self-love.

Take a moment to think about how you currently define yourself. Maybe you identify yourself as generous because you've had friends and family rave about the thoughtful gifts you given them over the years. Maybe you've even won an award for charity work in your local community. Perhaps being a talented artist is a part of your identity because your parents, teachers, and peers admired the drawings you created. Smart can be a part of your identity if you received good grades. Fashionable, if others often complimented the way you dressed. Funny, if you made the whole auditorium laugh during an ad-libbed line in a school play. Athletic, lucky, dedicated, strong, beautiful, talented, etc. can all be traits that become locked into how you view yourself.

While the good things seep into our identity, unfortunately, negative comments can stick in there as well. Babies aren't born thinking they're not good enough; if you feel critical of yourself, someone would have told you that in some way, shape, or form. Perhaps you label yourself as lazy because your parents called you lazy as a child every time you didn't want to help with chores. Maybe you labeled yourself as the weird kid because no one wanted to be your friend in elementary school. Maybe you think you're unattractive because a bully in high school told you so, but you never realized that bully was projecting their own insecurities because they were jealous of you. You took that bully's comments at face value and let it stick with you.

Everything you think about yourself, everything you've sewn into your identity, everything you've told yourself about the story of who you are and what's possible for you came from somewhere.

Your identity plays on a loop within your subconscious mind. It's constantly projecting the energetics of your identity into the Universe without you realizing. It's almost as if you're confirming your identity by having unknown affirmations on repeat such as "I am lucky," "I am friendly," "I am not smart enough," "I am not lovable."

The key here is to take the good parts of your identity and continue to let them empower you. Celebrate them! You absolutely are all those things and so much more. Then, take the parts of your identity that aren't serving you, understand where they came from, release them, and re-write them. Doing so will not only naturally help you manifest more of what you want, but it will also help you feel more confident, and when you feel more confident, you raise your internal vibration for self-love.

You can do these next two rituals – Rewriting Your Identity and the Fairy Tea Ceremony - back-to-back as they work in tandem with each other.

REWRITING YOUR IDENTITY

First, grab a piece of paper and write down unhelpful beliefs you currently have about yourself. I want you to be honest. No one will ever read this except you. List all the negative things you think about yourself. This list should include things you complain about regarding your physical appearance, personal qualities and capabilities, and who you are as a person.

Once you have your list, reflect upon each belief and ask yourself: Who told me these things were true?

Really think about it. Where did these negative thoughts originate? Did they come from your parent? A former partner? A peer? A boss? Society as a whole? At what age did you start to believe these stories to be true?

Think beyond yourself to identify when and where each listing belief came from. Ask Archangel Chamuel to help you find the origin point of each belief, of each part of your identity. Quiet your mind and have Chamuel pop a memory into your head. It might be a string of multiple memories; each memory having further solidified that same limiting belief within you.

Once you realize where those beliefs came from, consider: *Why does this person get to define any part of me? Why do they get to write my story?*

This is *your* story, and you can be whoever you say you are! If this belief came from someone else, it means it was learned, and if it was learned, it can be unlearned.

Next, make a list on a new page.

Quiet your mind, play meditation music, tune into your intuition, and ask your angels how they would describe you. Then connect with the fairies and ask them the same question. Finally, call in the mermaids and ask for their thoughts on who you are.

You can even take this exercise one step further by considering your soul, the soul that lovingly chose to incarnate as you. How would your soul describe you? What would they say your identity is? Think of all the positive parts of your identity you may have considered earlier. Include all those traits as well.

Once you have your new list, compare the two. You will immediately notice how they are incredibly different from each other. You'll also notice they *feel* differently. Your first list probably feels bad, right? That shows it's out of alignment with who you are. Our feelings are indicators of what is or isn't in harmony with us. The fact that your second list probably feels empowering shows that those parts of your identity align with who you are.

Now, consider who you want to trust. Who do you want to believe? The powerful and magical angels, fairies, and mermaids—or your mean boss, unhealed parent, or third-grade bully? It's an easy choice!

Now that we've figured out where those beliefs come from, it's time to let go of them and shred that old story so it is no longer our truth.

Take the first piece of paper, the one with the old, unwanted parts of your identity, and write on top of it: "These are not my truth. I release all forms of self-doubt. I release any negative thoughts toward myself. I release the need to battle with myself. I release judging myself. I release what others have told me I am."

Feel free to edit, replace, remove, or add anything to that list. Trust your intuition; trust what you feel called to write.

Then, I want you to carefully burn that piece of paper (in a safe location). Burn it outside either in a fire pit or a mini cast-iron cauldron. Thank the salamanders, the fire elementals, for igniting the fire and assisting you in burning away all that no longer serves you.

As you watch the paper burn, imagine all that negativity is burning away inside of you, allowing your heart to be clear and open.

Once it's finished burning, leave a gift, either some food or a fiery crystal, like carnelian, for the salamanders outside.

Then, I want you to look at the second list, the empowering one, and write on top of it: "These are my truths. I am choosing to believe in myself and my abilities. I am choosing to accept I am an incredible soul, inside and out. I am choosing to love and celebrate myself."

Again, feel free to edit, replace, remove, or add anything to that list. Trust your intuition; trust what you feel called to write.

Then, take this list and place it underneath a rose quartz crystal to infuse it with extra love. Every time you notice it in your room, allow it to be a reminder that you control your destiny, your fate, who you are, and how your life goes.

FAIRY TEA CEREMONY FOR SELF-LOVE

Another great technique for opening your heart and calling in more self-love is working with something you may already use on a daily basis: tea.

Tea is so magical because it's mainly water, and like everything in our Universe, water holds a strong, energetic vibration. This means you can program water with whatever energy you'd like via your words. Words are magic spells. The words we speak manifest into our reality, so speaking into our drinks allows the energetic vibration of those words to infuse into them, turning our drinks into a magical elixir. When we program our tea with magical intentions and then drink it, that energetic frequency is absorbed into our soul and helps that intent become our truth.

In this exercise, first create a magical fairy tea party atmosphere. Wear a vibrant outfit, play upbeat instrumental music, and surround yourself with crystals like rose quartz and unicorn stone. Bake or buy little treats like scones, mini cupcakes, and chocolate chip cookies. You can even hang up fairy lights.

Leave out an offering for the fairies, perhaps one of your treats, as you thank them for being with you today.

Brew yourself a cup of tea—any tea you'd like is fine, but a tea blend with ingredients like rose and strawberry vibrates closely with the natural energy of love. To connect more with the fairies, you can add ingredients fairies love like butterfly pea tea and honey.

Think back to the list you created in the previous exercise, about the empowering identity you acknowledged, and all the words you want to be true about yourself. Create a list of affirmations that mirror your list.

Write things like: *I am lovable; I am magical; I am stunning; I am kind; I am talented; I am more than good enough; I love myself; I radiate pure love inside and out.*

Once your tea has cooled slightly at drinking temperature, hold the cup in your hands and feel your palms vibrating with the energy of self-love. Feel all the love you have for yourself radiating from your heart and extending into your tea. Ask your fairies to be with you and guide you, as you speak all your affirmations into your tea.

Then take a sip of your tea and feel all those positive, empowering words being absorbed into your soul. Imagine your heart chakra opening wider and wider as you feel all the love and gratitude you have for yourself. Visualize the tea as a beautiful, shimmering light of rose gold moving from your mouth, down your throat, and to your belly with each sip. Feel that fairy magic vibrating through you. Feel your words flowing through you, becoming a part of you, becoming your truth, magnetizing you to love.

Continue this process until your tea is finished. Speak your words, sip the tea, and feel them absorb into your energy and become your truth.

When you are finished, thank your fairies, and enjoy the rest of your delicious tea party.

You can do a simpler version of this ritual every single day with any kind of drink you have. Just speak your intentions into your cup and drink! It's powerful yet simple and sure to continually help you radiate with self-love.

IN YOUR OWN TIME

Take your self-love journey day by day. There's no reason to rush. You have the rest of your life to see, appreciate, and fall in love with the amazing, one-of-a-kind soul that is you!

Just as we each have an individual timeline for finding romantic love, we also have our own timeline for cultivating self-love. It's a process that has no deadline. Treat yourself like a plant. So long as you are willing to put in the effort to water, nurture, and bring sunshine to yourself, that's what matters most.

As you're working through the self-love exercises in this book, take your time with them. Don't feel pressured to check them off your to-do list. Self-love requires patience. If any of the self-love exercises in this book feel too uncomfortable, redoing previous exercises and working through them again may help. You can repeat any of them as often as you'd like or anytime you need.

Overall, you're doing great. Be proud of yourself for simply being a willing participant on this journey. You are a beautiful soul and deserve to fall in love with yourself deeply.

I especially love working with the mermaids to increase my self-love. If there is anyone who knows how to appreciate their inner and outer beauty, it's the mermaids. I have a personal mermaid guide and she goes the extra mile to hype me up whenever I need it. (And I honestly love hyping her up back! It's a mutual hype session and feels so uplifting). Mermaids make self-love seem so effortless as they have no hangups with proudly celebrating themselves.

We often shy away from outwardly loving ourselves as society labels those who do as conceited, self-absorbed, or even selfish. While we don't want to come across as vain, it's important to normalize complimenting yourself. It's okay to have a healthy dose of love and to be your own hype friend whenever you need!

There's a difference between conceit and confidence. Conceit is loudly bragging about oneself, most often to mask high levels of insecurity. Confidence is proudly showing up as 100% you, knowing your worth, and not letting anyone else's opinions make you question yourself. The mermaids are experts at helping you feel the latter.

With this next exercise, you'll be sitting down in front of the mirror, and allowing the mermaids to work their magic to help you become as confident as they are.

MERMAID MIRROR WORK

Mermaids adore hyping you up and allowing you to see the true beauty in yourself. A fantastic way to cultivate that inner love for yourself is through Mermaid Mirror Work.

This exercise is simple, all you need is a mirror of any size. If you decide to use a handheld mirror, decorate it with seashells and ocean trinkets. If you're using a mounted wall mirror or a vanity mirror, decorate the surrounding area with your shells and trinkets.

Before you begin, light a sea-scented candle, play ocean sounds, and hold onto an aquamarine crystal. Feel free to also dress up in your most mermaid-inspired outfit. This could be wearing summer attire, the colors of the ocean, or anything sparkly and romantic.

Take a deep breath and look into the mirror. Look deeply into your own eyes. It may be uncomfortable at first, but try not to look away. Hold your own gaze. Clear your mind, call upon the mermaids, and ask them to help reflect the true beauty within you. Ask them to help you notice all the ways you sparkle and shine. Start to see yourself with fresh eyes, with the eyes of the mermaids.

Tune into your intuition and notice what compliments pop into your mind.

Spend at least five minutes doing this. It may seem difficult at first, especially if you're not used to showing yourself love, but please persevere. Keep complimenting yourself, appreciating yourself, and showing yourself love. The more frequently you do this exercise, the easier it will become.

When you're finished, send yourself overflowing gratitude. Spend time feeling genuinely grateful that you are you. Thank the mermaids for their help and offer them a trinket as a token of your thanks.

WALKING YOUR OWN PATH

When it comes to self-love, try not to be so hard on yourself. You are doing the best you can—we all are! You may not have always had it easy, but you are working through your challenges, which is admirable and amazing. Yes, you may have had more obstacles to overcome than others, but it doesn't mean you are any less worthy and deserving of your happily ever after.

You are not behind. You didn't mess up or go off path. There's no set schedule for when you need to achieve things, nor do you even need to achieve certain things at all. How boring would it be if we all experienced the exact same life story? Imagine if we all looked the same, acted the same, and had the same talents? That would certainly that take the magic and excitement out of everything.

We're all beautifully unique and wonderfully different so, of course, our stories are going to be different. Of course, our timelines are going to be different. You're exactly on time, and you're exactly where you need to be for *you*.

Don't fight yourself wishing you could've, would've, or should've. Everything in your life has served a purpose. If you look back in hindsight, you can recognize all the lessons you've learned, especially from the things that didn't work out.

The path you're on, the one you've been on, is always the path meant for you. See the beauty in your growth, and appreciate your journey because life isn't about the destination; it's about the experience. Experiencing it all—the ups and downs, the triumphs and victories, feeling the surprise, the excitement, the tears, the love, all of it—is part of humanity. It's why we're here! Just being human and experiencing life is our purpose.

Be gentle with yourself. It's okay if your life doesn't look as you imagined it. Going forward, you absolutely have the power to change that and to make your life the magical one you've always dreamed about. You do that by being authentically you, the beautiful being your soul chose to be.

You are unique. You are one-of-a-kind. There are billions of people on this planet and only one you—how special is that? Start to accept that you are a gorgeous, intelligent, funny, talented, amazing, worthy, brilliant human being just because you're *you*!

You are magnificent, you are fabulous, you are powerful, and most of all, you are magical. Feel all that magic surging through you, and know that you have the power to create anything—truly, anything. You exist for a reason, and the fact that you exist right here, right now, means there's still a plan for you. You are divinely beautiful, you are superbly special, and you are so incredibly loved.

Feel it, believe it, and know it!

Releasing the Past

You can't manifest love without truly letting go of the past and releasing everything that no longer serves you. When you surrender and let go, you create space to *finally* move forward.

What happened in your love life's past is no indication of what will happen in the future. Just because it hasn't worked out for you so far doesn't mean it will keep going that way.

Imagine yourself breaking that pattern of unsuccessful romantic endeavors and imagine yourself stepping into a beautiful light filled with happiness and love. Open your heart to receive beautiful love.

You are ready!
Step into
that energy
of knowing
it is yours.

Accept that in the eyes of the Universe, there are no mistakes in your past—even though it may feel like there are. Everything you've experienced in your romantic history had a lesson that helped your soul develop and grow. Even if the lesson was learning what you didn't want, how to stand up for yourself, or deciding to never, ever settle, it still provided you with something vital to your soul's growth.

In hindsight, I can see clearly how all my experiences in romance, even the difficulties, taught me something important. While it was painful at the time, the heartaches and breaks gave me clarity, strength, and wisdom. I was then able to take that wisdom into future relationships. It also allowed me to help my friends heal their heartbreaks and teach them that they deserve the purest love. Eventually, those lessons assisted me in understanding and guiding clients and students in my classes, too.

However, in cases of deeply traumatic relationship experiences, such as abuse, it is not appropriate to say, "everything happens for a reason." I'm so sorry if anything like that happened to you, but just know it was never your fault. While traumatic experiences may not ever be forgivable, you deserve not to let that person or those people hold energetic power over you any longer. Karma will handle them.

You deserve to reclaim your own power and personal peace, move forward, and know it is always, always, *always* still possible for you to have the best life and best love story.

Your past doesn't have to define you; only you can define yourself. Don't be afraid to speak out or even use your story to help others who have gone through similar situations; we've all seen the ripple effect that can create.

You are a beautiful soul who has been dealt a hard hand, and I send you the strength and love needed to move forward and find ways to create your happily ever after because you absolutely deserve that (and always have).

CLARITY LIST

When it comes to manifesting, it's best to be as clear as possible to the Universe. You want to let it know what you are energetically available for in love and what you are *not* energetically available for in love.

Take out your journal or a piece of paper and draw a line down the center of the page.

On one side of the line, write: "I am energetically available for…" and on the other side, write: "I am NOT energetically available for…"

Then, fill each column with all the details that resonate with you. Again, leaning into what you don't want will help you gain clarity on what you *do* want. For example, if you recognize you don't want a partner who will flirt with others, write that on your NOT list, but also put "someone who is loyal" under your FOR list.

Once you have both sides completed, cut the page in half to separate your lists.

Hold your NOT list and passionately declare to the Universe out loud, "I am not energetically available for any of this!" Then tear up the paper, safely burn it, or just throw it out entirely as a symbolic gesture that it is not meant for you.

Set your rules. The Universe will listen.

Then, take your FOR list and write it all down in one combined paragraph. Example: "I am energetically available for a partner who is romantic and kind, who loves watching movies with me, who thinks astrology is cool, who likes going on bike rides, who is witty and clever, who supports me in all I do." Make this paragraph as rich and detailed as you desire.

Finish by writing: "Thank you for all of this or something better!" The Universe *may* have something wonderful in mind that wasn't on your list. Declaring "this or something better" keeps you open to the magic.

Of course, keep in mind if a potential love interest appears and they do not match all your qualities exactly, it does not mean they're automatically not the love of your life. You never want to settle on major things that are important to you, like a partner who is loyal or family-oriented. However, with the small things, be open. Certain traits don't necessarily have to be dealbreakers and may even change over time.

Maybe your dream partner loves astrology as much as you do, and that's super important to you because it's your line of work. However, you meet someone who doesn't know what house their Sun is in or what that even means. This doesn't instantly indicate they're not the one because you wrote "must love astrology" on your list. For all you know, just because they don't know about it *yet* doesn't mean they won't love it in time. Maybe you're the one meant to introduce them to it, and when they learn about it, they may become just as passionate about it as you are. Maybe, they never understand astrology, but they are incredibly supportive, cheer you on, and honor your passion for it.

Maybe you never thought you'd enjoy surfing, but you date someone who's super into catching waves, so you give it a try and realize it's a lot of fun. Maybe you try surfing and are horrible at it, but it makes you realize you love photographing surfers and that ignites a new passion within you. Keep yourself open to little surprises like that because you seriously never know.

Now, this isn't about changing people. We definitely don't want to change people or change ourselves. It's about being open to people's evolution and our own evolution. For the small things, give them a chance. They might turn out to adore your interests, just as you might turn out to love theirs.

It's also okay if you never have the same interests; as long as you are supportive of each other's likes, dislikes, and individual autonomy, that's still a good match. But if someone is dismissive of your passions or doesn't align with the non-negotiables that *really* matter to you, then, of course, it's okay to move on. Be grateful that an option manifested, but show the Universe you are serious about what you want and don't want.

Sometimes, we do receive what we don't want as a way of the Universe checking: *Do you truly believe this is possible for you? Or are you going to just settle?*

Show the Universe you do believe! It's like missing a train. You wouldn't panic and think no train is ever going to come again, and you're stranded at the station forever. You'd just patiently wait for the next one because you *know* another one is coming along soon, and there are many other options to reach your destination. It may not come as quickly as you'd like, but another train will show up sooner or later and work out perfectly for you.

HEALING FROM HEARTBREAK

If you're currently heartbroken, be gentle with yourself. There is no set timetable for healing. Your feelings are perfectly valid and real; it's okay not to be okay. Heartbreak is a loss; your soul is grieving what could have been.

This anonymous quote that circled around the internet helped me in the past: "If you were able to love someone completely wrong for you, just imagine how much deeper you'll be able to love someone completely right for you."

The fact that your heart was broken shows that you're capable of loving. Don't let someone who didn't deserve you ruin any part of your experience of love. It will be okay, you will heal, and you'll be stronger and wiser because of it.

Try not to take rejection so personally; feel comfortable accepting it. Some people like wine; some hate it. Some people love cheese; some people can't digest it. People just have different preferences, and it has no reflection upon you. Just because you're not one particular person's dream partner doesn't mean you're not beautiful, amazing, and worthy. It doesn't mean someone else won't think you are the most incredible soul they've ever met.

How someone else feels about you does not determine your worth. Another person's opinion is simply that, just their opinion, not a fact. Despite what the world tends to think, opinions are not facts.

Only *you* can determine your worth, and the fact that you exist right here, right now, as you means the Universe thinks you're worthy enough to be here.

For healing heartbreak, I love using affirmations. When I needed to heal my heart in the past, stating affirmations out loud or even just writing them down in my own handwriting made me feel like I was taking back my power and re-writing my story.

Over time, the more you work with affirmations, the more your brain starts to accept them as your truth, and your energy begins to match the frequency of the words you are saying.

Here are some of my favorite affirmations to help heal from heartbreak:

- *I am worthy of love. I am amazing just because I'm me.*
- *I am strong. I can handle anything. I can get through anything.*
- *I allow myself time and space to heal.*

- *I trust my path. I have faith in the Universe and know I'm always being led to the best outcomes.*
- *I am beautiful. I am gorgeous. I am stunning on the outside, and I am just as fabulous on the inside.*
- *I'm an amazing, strong, powerful, beautiful, wonderful human being. I'm grateful to be me.*
- *I am the only one who determines my worth, and I am worthy simply because I'm me.*

One of the best things I ever did was forgive—forgive everyone in my romantic past and forgive myself. When we hold onto anger and regret, all it does is clog up our energetic field. It stays in our aura and blocks that new, aligned, happy-in-love energy from flowing in.

When I decided to get serious about changing my love mindset to call in my true love, I developed an exercise for releasing, healing, and letting go of my romantic past, and it changed everything. It helped me in more ways than I could ever fully express and opened my heart to receive my true love soon afterward.

Less than a month after I created and did this upcoming exercise, things finally came together to have my first date with my true love. We've been together ever since.

I think it's no coincidence that even though I had known him for almost two years at that point, things hadn't aligned for us to be together romantically until *after* I did this exercise to energetically clear out my past. It absolutely paved the way for me to be ready to handle that kind of love in my life. It reset my energy and leveled up my soul.

This is arguably the most important exercise in this entire book, so please don't skip over it!

ARCHANGEL FULL MOON RITUAL

The full moon is the best time of the month to let things go—and have them *stay* let go! At this time, the moon is completely illuminated in all its divinity, so it helps us shine a light on what is no longer working for us. Specifically, it shines a light on what energy we are still holding onto in our lives that prevents us from manifesting what we want.

Archangel Haniel, the angel of intuition and divine feminine energy, is my go-to during this time. Since she is associated with the moon (the moon is the ultimate symbol of divine feminine energy) calling upon her for any moon-releasing ritual will add that extra boost of magic.

Look up the next full moon on your calendar, and plan to do this ritual when it comes along. Once it's the full moon, ask Archangel Haniel to be with you as you write letters to all of your exes.

Everything that happened or didn't happen with our previous partners, or even just crushes, can linger within our energetic field. Just as you can't add new clothes to a full closet without removing the old ones that no longer fit, you can't manifest new love without fully letting go of old loves. If you are serious about calling in the love of your life, energetically clearing out your past is the most important step you can take.

On the night of the full moon, make a list of all your former romantic partners you can think of. Feel free to include anyone you've ever been in a relationship with, gone on a date with, or had some kind of romantic connection or loving feelings toward, even if it was unrequited. You can also include a longtime crush that never progressed as well as casual romantic experiences.

Then, with Archangel Haniel's support, I want you to go through each of them one at a time and write them a letter, detailing anything and everything you need to get off your chest. You can either write to these people individually, or write a collective letter to the group as a whole. Don't worry, you aren't going to send this letter. This is more metaphorical for you to get those feelings out of your system, so don't hold back.

Once you've completed your letter, I want you to imagine giving it to Archangel Haniel. Visualize Haniel delivering your letter to the bright, full moon and allowing the illumination, the beaming light of the celestial body, to completely encompass the letter. Know that the moon's light will completely resolve and heal this situation, supporting you to finally let it all go.

Bask in the vibrant, healing light of Haniel and the full moon. Let this light fill every inch of your soul, healing you from head to toe.

After that, your next step is to consider these relationships and identify the lessons you learned from your experiences.

Maybe you learned that you deserve better and shouldn't settle. Maybe you learned to stand up for yourself. Maybe you learned that you are capable of loving. Maybe you learned an important life skill. Maybe this relationship was a positive one, and it led you to make an impactful choice or study something that improved your life.

This process will not only help you find closure in the situation, as it allows you to recognize there was a reason you went down this path, but it also tells the Universe that you truly accept that everything has a purpose in your divine soul's growth.

After you've recognized your lessons from these relationships, thank the other person involved in your head. Wish them well on their journey. Hope that they find the love of their life, if they haven't already. Send them blessings because that's how *you win.* That's how you get them out of your energy field, and that's how you clear space to open your heart again to receive the love of your life. Send them forgiveness and maybe even say sorry yourself. Sometimes, we have to admit our own role in the situation. Accepting accountability on our part for any failings can lead to growth and healing.

Please know, in the case of abuse, you don't have to thank that person, wish them well, or forgive them. That's on them. Just pray that they recognize the horrors of what they've done and find healing. You don't deserve to let them take any more of your peace.

Once you've done that, call upon Archangel Michael, the protector angel, and ask him to help cut any energetic cords that are no longer needed. We all have energetic cords that connect us with those we have strong emotional ties to. Remember when you were little and would play silly field games at school or camp—those games where you were tied to someone and tasked with completing a challenge together? Remember how hard it was to move being tied to someone else? This is why it's great to call upon

Michael to cut the cords. If we are tangled up in the energetic cords of others, it's hard to move forward. Michael helps us break free.

Some cords are connected via karmic loops and patterns and may need to remain intact as it is a necessary lesson in your soul's evolution. Some previous relationships are more complicated than others and can't simply be cut. Perhaps you co-parent with your ex or still work closely with a former partner through your job. In these cases, it's great to ask Archangel Michael to remove *only* parts of the relationship that no longer serve you and are not necessary for karmic lessons. If this person still needs to be in your life, Ask Michael to remove any tension (if there is any) so you can have peace and harmony moving forward in your experience with them.

Imagine Michael using his mighty sword and severing only unhealthy and unnecessary connections between you and your ex as you *finally*, energetically release what has been holding you back. After doing so, you may feel much lighter and overcome with a new sense of freedom.

Finally, call upon Archangel Raphael, the healing angel, to send healing, love, and light to you, your former partner, and all involved. Visualize shimmering, green light surrounding you, your past, your former partner, and the situation. Once again, wish everyone well and know what happened in the past can no longer effect you.

Repeat this process, working with Haniel, Michael, and Raphael, going through any and all former romantic partners in turn.

A beautiful future in love is ahead of you, wide open and ready.

FORGIVENESS

While you're forgiving your exes, of course, don't forget to forgive yourself.

How many times have you looked back and thought: *I knew I shouldn't have dated them; I never should have trusted them; I wish I never met them; I wish I had been smarter; I wish I could turn back time; I wish, I wish…*

Maybe you feel at fault because you allowed yourself to be hurt or misled, or you seemingly made foolish choices you'd do anything to take back. Maybe you feel guilty that you hurt someone good. It's great to take responsibility and hold ourselves accountable for the times *we* contributed to the problem as well.

No matter what regrets you're facing, know that you're not alone; we all have these thoughts at times. However, they can interfere with our ability to manifest.

Remind yourself that you can't change the past. No matter what you do, there's no way to turn back time. So, you have two options. You can either cling to reliving and regretting the past, *or* you can choose to no longer let that chapter of your life define you. You have the power to release the hold it has over you, allowing you to move forward toward the life you want and the love you want.

If you had known better at the time, you would've done better. Back then, you may have chosen your heart, which is more admirable than foolish. Recognizing now that you wish you had chosen differently shows that you've grown, and that's exactly what you're supposed to be doing. Your whole life purpose is to learn and grow.

The fact that you understand more and see things more clearly now means you received the lesson. It means you're making great use of your time here in Earth School and evolving.

SELF-FORGIVENESS WITH YOUR HIGHER SELF AND ARCHANGEL MICHAEL

No matter the reason, if you need to forgive yourself for anything, this exercise will help you release the pain of holding onto the past.

In this meditation, you are going to connect with your Higher Self.

Each of us has a Higher Self. Our Higher Self is essentially our soul. They're the version of us who see things from a grander perspective. They're not bogged down by all the human emotions and human problems; they are pure, unconditional love and understanding. They've lived lifetimes and are the wisest version of you.

Your Higher Self is amazing to work with for self-forgiveness as they have a deeper level of understanding of each situation. They have the purest point of view and can help "Earth you" see that as well.

We'll also be connecting with Archangel Michael in this meditation as he helps us release anything heavy we are still holding onto.

As with any meditation, set the mood. Use essential oil, burn a candle, and hold onto crystals. In this case, I recommend rose quartz for self-love and angelite for both forgiveness and connection with Archangel Michael.

Scan the QR code to download and listen to the audio version of this meditation found at the back of this book.

Take a deep breath in and a deep breath out.

Take a deep breath in and a deep breath out.

Imagine you begin to ascend. You are lifting off the ground. As you rise into the sky, you notice beautiful white, fluffy clouds stretching out for miles and miles in every direction. Sparkling sunlight twinkles through the clouds, illuminating everything around you.

Up here, everything is peaceful and serene.

You float slightly downwards and realize you can stand on the clouds; they support you perfectly.

As you stand on the clouds, you start to feel their beautiful, light energy filling you up, from bottom to top.

Beautiful white light begins to cleanse and clear every inch of your body, cleansing all your chakra points and extending into your aura.

The white light removes anything that's bothering you, dissolves it, and fills you up with pure serenity and peace. You feel good. You feel whole.

You especially feel the white light travel into your heart as it washes away anything heavy, anything that's bothering you. Those blocks dissolve now as your heart absorbs that beautiful, white light.

You feel loved. You feel supported.

You are safe. You are protected.

You will now only interact with spirits of the highest level of light and love, with the purest intention for all involved.

You feel a beautiful, enlightened, magical, warming presence coming toward you.

Much like your newly cleansed heart, they, too, feel filled with pure love and pure light.

As they get closer, you realize it's Archangel Michael, and he's smiling at you.

Michael approaches and stands next to you, gently letting you know he will be by your side this entire time. He is here to help you connect with your Higher Self, to help you forgive, to let go of anything you're still holding onto, and to move forward confidently full of love.

You turn to Archangel Michael and thank him.

And now, you ask him, "May I speak with my Higher Self? I want to have an honest conversation with myself about anything I need to forgive so I may move forward."

Archangel Michael nods. He extends his hand away from you and clasps another hand, pulling forward your Higher Self.

Your Higher Self now stands before you,

They look exactly like you, just covered head to toe in golden, radiant energy.

You can feel all the love and magic within. They are the best, most aligned version of your soul. Your Higher Self smiles at you as Archangel Michael stands by both of your sides.

Have a conversation with your Higher Self. Ask them, "What do I need to forgive myself for so that I can move forward?"

Allow this conversation to unfold for as long as you need.

Once you feel you have finished this conversation, thank your Higher Self for their help and honesty.

Together, you and your Higher Self turn to Archangel Michael, and with a wave of his sword, he cuts away any guilt, resentment, fear, and low energies that you have been holding onto or directing toward yourself.

You feel these lower energies leaving your body and being replaced with golden sparkling light.

You turn to your Higher Self, grab their hands, and say, "I forgive you. I forgive me."

Your Higher Self looks at you and smiles as they, too, say, "I forgive you. I forgive me."

Feel limitless love for your Higher Self. Feel that limitless love for yourself too, as you are one.

Thank your Higher Self for their help and thank Archangel Michael for their help.

Know you can continue to connect with both of them for more forgiveness work whenever you wish.

For now, it is time to return to your body. Imagine yourself descending through the clouds, through the sky, back into your body, fully grounded, and sitting upon the Earth.

And when you're ready, you may open your eyes.

Feel free to journal about your experience in this meditation.

As we just were in the clouds working with our Higher Self, who has an extremely high vibe, I recommend holding onto a grounding crystal like smokey quartz or black tourmaline to bring your energy back into your body. Place your feet firmly on the ground and imagine roots extending from them and connecting you to the divine core of Mother Earth. This is also your excuse to eat some dark chocolate, as that will also help ground your energy after vibrating so highly.

Be proud of yourself for doing this work. It isn't easy, but it will be so worth it. You're incredible, and as you go forward, make sure you see that! Be kinder to yourself, forgive yourself when you need to, and come back to this exercise any time you wish to let some things go and understand yourself a little more.

SOUL MATES, KARMIC LOOPS, AND TWIN FLAMES

Sometimes, no matter how much healing we do, the problem still persists. It does so because the roots of certain issues may not necessarily lie in this current lifetime but stem from another lifetime, a previous incarnation.

Perhaps you don't believe in reincarnation—the idea that our soul returns in a new body across multiple lifetimes— and that's okay. You might also be unsure of your beliefs about past lives. If the upcoming past life exploration exercise does not resonate with you, feel free to skip it. However, I encourage you to read through this section with an open mind, in case something speaks to you. Even if you view it as an imaginative experiment, exploring past lives is a valuable approach to uncovering blocks around romance.

As souls, we are always spiritually evolving, on a journey that extends through multiple lifetimes. You've had several lifetimes before this one, just as you'll most likely have many more after this one. The problem (or blessing) is that with each incarnation, we tend to forget the entirety of our previous ones. It's as if we have amnesia, and all the events that happened slip out of our minds. This happens as a protective measure because if you remembered every detail of all of your lifetimes, all your identities,
all at once,
you'd be very,
very confused.

However, we often have fragments of those lifetimes pop in. We may have certain inclinations toward certain parts of the world and time periods in history; we may find ourselves more naturally talented at certain things. Maybe you somehow understand French despite never having taken a French class. Maybe you are inexplicably drawn to Shakespeare's plays. Maybe you love the era of the samurai. Maybe in school, you just happened to know every answer on a test about the Aztecs without studying. Maybe you yearn for the Hawaiian Islands. Maybe growing up, you had a talent for oil painting. Maybe you have a knack for cooking the most delicious Indian cuisine. Maybe you pick up the harp and can play it intuitively. All of these can be considered evidence that points to where, when, and who you were in your past life.

We carry over good things, like our talents and affinities. However, we also carry over not-so-good things like our traumatic experiences. While our conscious mind forgets our past lives, our subconscious mind stores all the details.

Perhaps you have a fear of the ocean in this lifetime but have never had a traumatic incident around water. In a past life, you may have lived in Atlantis and still carry soul memories of the oceanic destruction of that advanced civilization.

Fears and blocks that have no origin story in this lifetime can almost always be pinpointed to a past life. An unexplained fear of abandonment may stem from being an orphan in a previous existence. A fear of rejection may stem from a lover breaking your heart and betraying you. Constant difficulties with dating may derive from a past life where you took a vow of chastity as a high priestess.

I learned a block in my love life stemmed from a past life where I had been forced to marry someone I did not love. For a while in this lifetime, I felt that something was wrong with me because I didn't like the people who were romantically interested in me. I felt scared that I might never find someone *I* loved who also loved me in return. Uncovering this past life and recognizing where these feelings originated helped me heal that fear.

I then was able to discover several past lives where I *did* happily fall in love and marry by choice, proving to myself that my soul *was* capable of true love. I then adopted the belief that if it happened in previous lifetimes, *of course,* it could happen again in this lifetime. (And you know it did!)

As you decide to embark on uncovering your past lives,

know they don't have to all be dark and scary. You also have access to view the wonderful fulfilling ones. I like to guide my clients through seeing fun past lives because that helps them, too. Our previous incarnations can also support us in showing us that we *did* have magical, happily ever afters. It's proof that things *do* just magically work out in some lifetimes.

While the fun lifetimes are great to see, it is important to not get caught up in them, and to allow yourself to tap into the more difficult past lives, as well. I always guide my clients through seeing both. We need balance. Just as the joyful lifetimes uplift us, the more challenging ones are where we learn the most and also offer the greatest opportunities for healing.

No matter the details of what happened and regardless of its intensity, the imprint of a past life event still exists within your energy. If the issue isn't resolved or healed, it will travel with you and affect your current lifetime and all lifetimes to come until it is healed. That's why, in terms of manifesting love, past life regression can be a breakthrough, helping you to explore the energetic imprints you are carrying within your soul.

Some of the past life lessons we need to heal will involve the same key players. We tend to incarnate within the same group of souls. This means your true love in this lifetime most likely was your love interest in a previous lifetime. Just the same, your best friend in this lifetime could've been your sister; your parent most likely was once your child. We stay within the same soul family, but we change roles. That's why people, especially our romantic interests, often seem familiar because we've known them for centuries in some cases.

All of these people you incarnate with are known as your soulmates. Yes, soulmates aren't exclusive to just romantic partners; soulmates are everyone you consistently choose to reincarnate with. It's your whole soul group.

As you are working through your past lives, don't be surprised if you show up as a different gender or ethnicity or if someone you currently know shows up in a completely different body. Throughout your lifetimes, you'll switch appearances and ethnicities, and you'll also switch genders to understand reality through different perspectives. Like the archangels, our natural souls have a balance of energies, so we will have some lifetimes as a woman, some as a man, and some as non-binary neutral souls.

As I briefly mentioned earlier, some souls are connected via karmic cycles or loops. A karmic cycle is one where you repeat lessons over and over again, oftentimes switching roles, until you *finally* learn your lessons and understand them from a higher perspective.

For example, in love, maybe you and a certain soul are caught in a karmic loop where one of you keeps cheating on the other, and then, as a result of the betrayal, one soul wants revenge. The loop will end when both souls rise above these experiences and make different choices—where they forget cheating or forget revenge, forgive the other, wish them well, and move on.

I also want to take a moment to mention "twin flames" here. There are always so many questions on this topic. People have come to think of the term twin flame as synonymous with “the one,” a cosmic soul that they are bound to, their other half. They’ve become romanticized and glorified, but twin flames are incredibly toxic. They’re not your other half; they’re your mirror. They will reflect back everything you are lacking, just as you will reflect that back to them. Twin flames are almost always triggering. Twin flame relationships are volatile and tumultuous as they are meant to challenge you, push you, and make you uncomfortable.

A twin flame is not something you want to manifest; *a soulmate, yes*, but a twin flame can literally turn your world upside-down and not in a good way. We don’t interact with our twin flames in every lifetime, and they are not always a romantic partner. Sometimes, they’re not even a gender you’re attracted to; sometimes, they are a friend, a parent, a family member, a mentor, etc. Sometimes, they are someone you instantly do not like and never like.

As you are doing your past life regressions, you could notice a particular triggering soul continually popping up, and that may indicate the presence of a twin flame. Just know they are not your one true love.

We’ve each had so many lifetimes here on Earth and potentially on other planets as well. During your regression you may experience yourself in a world that looks nothing like any landscape here on Earth. Trust it. You may also find yourself living a lifetime in a fairy or mermaid realm. Trust that as well. Be open to whatever comes through.

There’s no limit to how much past life work you can do, as there’s always more to learn, understand, and heal.

ARCHANGEL RAZIEL PAST LIFE DISCOVERY

Archangel Raziel is the archangel who helps guide us through our past lives. He helps us understand our souls and journeys on a deeper level.

For this exercise, we are going to work with Archangel Raziel via meditation and automatic writing to understand our romantic experiences from past lives. This will definitely give you a deeper level of healing and understanding of why you've been experiencing love the way you have been.

I recommend doing this exercise several times over the course of several weeks (every other week would be great to give yourself time to process and understand) because there is always a lot to learn from many different incarnations. In this meditation, we'll be asking Raziel to show us the biggest factor from our past lives that is affecting us now.

Connecting with Raziel to show you your past life relationships with previous partners from this life is also recommended to understand why certain relationships unfolded the way they did—and that's something you can also do in this meditation.

First, you'll close your eyes and meditate (as guided below), see the past life, and then you're going to come out of the meditation and use a technique called automatic writing.

Automatic writing is the process of stream-of-consciousness journaling: just scribbling down anything and everything that comes to mind. When connecting with Archangel Raziel, it'll be as if Archangel Raziel is speaking through you, guiding you with answers.

After meditating, you'll be led to ask certain questions. Write those down on your paper first, and then ask Raziel to answer the questions, and instantly write down whatever pops into your head.

The key to automatic writing is to trust whatever is coming to you. You are highly intuitive and more than capable of connecting. I promise you are *not* making anything up. Whatever is coming to you is coming to you for a reason.

If you find yourself struggling to receive these intuitive messages, try just writing out your thoughts, anything that comes to mind, even if it's "I really wish I could do this," just keep writing. Write down the things you hear, see, and feel. Write down things you notice in your room. Just put pen to page and, soon enough, you'll slip into that state where Spirit can write through you!

As you allow Raziel's words to flow through you, your handwriting and dialect may change. You may notice it comes across as a higher level of speaking; angels like to use kind words like "beloved," "my darling," etc. Always read back what you wrote afterward because you may not necessarily remember having written it, as it was being channeled from the angelic realm.

To enhance your intuition, make sure you set the mood while doing this exercise. Light some candles, dim the lights, use lavender essential oil, play meditation music, and surround yourself with some intuition-boosting crystals like amethyst and selenite.

I also highly recommend using lapis lazuli during this exercise, as it is my favorite crystal for connecting to past lives.

Scan the QR code to download and listen to the audio version of this meditation found at the back of this book.

Take a deep breath in and a deep breath out.

Take a deep breath in and a deep breath out.

Know you are a powerful, beautiful, wonderful being. You are made up of all the same magic as the Universe, the sun, the stars, and the moon. All that power exists in you.

You are a divine child of the Universe, and you are more than capable of anything just by being you.

Feel love and gratitude for all that you are, all that you have been throughout all your lifetimes, and all that you will be.

Breathe in. Breathe out.

Now, imagine nighttime skies of blue and purple surrounding you. Vivid, twinkling stars, shimmering constellations. You feel safe. You feel empowered. You can feel all the magic.

Magic surrounds you. Magic is within you. Magic is you.

You feel your crown chakra glowing, opening wider and wider, as a beautiful beam of light is sent down from Spirit right to you. It enters through your crown chakra, bringing with it all the wisdom of the Universe and a deep connection to Spirit, enhancing your intuition.

The white light makes its way down your forehead, lighting up your third eye. You can now see further and deeper and see beautiful, spiritual truths and all aspects of your previous lives.

The white light makes its way down to your ears, allowing you to hear Spirit clearly and precisely.

The white light fills up your nose and your mouth. Then it makes its way down to your throat, opening your throat chakra, allowing you to speak freely with Spirit and channel their wise words.

The white light makes its way down your shoulders and into your heart. It fills your heart with beautiful white light so you can feel all the love the Universe has for you.

The white light goes down your arms, your hands, and fingers.

It fills up your chest, your ribs, your stomach. It fills up your solar plexus chakra, allowing you to trust your gut feelings and trust the messages you will be receiving.

The white light fills up your sacral chakra, connecting you to brilliant solutions, understanding and unlocking them on a deeper level.

The white light makes its way to your root chakra, grounding you. The white light fills your thighs, your knees, your calves, and your feet.

You are now filled with only beautiful, radiant energy.

Finally, Spirit sends more energy through to your crown chakra so that you are encased in a beautiful bubble of white light.

You are safe; you are protected. You will now only interact with Spirit of the highest level of light and the purest intention for all involved.

You are highly intuitive. You are connected. You are capable.

Now, you see a beautiful rainbow light coming toward you. It's energy of the highest vibration of love. You don't feel afraid; you feel completely at ease, like reuniting with an old friend.

As the rainbow light gets closer and closer, the form shifts into the radiant figure of an angel. It's Archangel Raziel, and they are here to assist you today.

Now, tell Raziel you'd like to understand deeper truths about your romantic experiences and your love life in all your lifetimes.

Here, you have several options: You can ask him to show you what is the most important past life, the most relevant past life to now, or ask him to show you a lifetime where you need to heal something in order to move forward in your love life in your current lifetime. You may also ask him to show you the relationship dynamics between you and a particular soul in order to better understand and move forward. Or you may ask him to show you a lifetime where love did work out for you to prove to you that it is also possible in this lifetime.

Whatever you feel you need to focus on today, trust it, and ask Archangel Raziel to bring it all to you now.

Raziel smiles wide at you and is ready to help you understand these aspects of your past lives to make sense of this current life, to help you heal, to help you move forward, and to live a magical existence in love.

Raziel reaches out and lovingly holds one of your hands with his and places their other hand on your third eye. Raziel's rainbow aura extends into you. As you start to see, as you start to feel, as you start to know . . .

Archangel Raziel fills you with the knowledge of your past lives.

Allow the scene to start to unfold before you, and ask yourself these questions:

Are you in a particular era in time?

What part of the world does this feel like?

Are you viewing this scene from inside your own body—and if so, what kind of body are you in? What gender are you? What ethnicity are you?

Or are you viewing this as an outside observer?

How do you feel right now? Joyful? Fearful? Angry? Excited?

Is anyone else with you? Do they feel like certain souls you've met before?

What scene is playing before you?

What do you feel this experience is trying to tell you?

Allow this to go on for as long as you need, and then when you're ready . . .

Take a deep breath in and a deep breath out.

On the count of five, you're going to slowly come back to your room, still connected with Archangel Raziel, still connected to this past life, and you are going to write down anything and everything you feel coming to you.

1 . . . 2 . . .3 . . .4 . . .5 . . .

Wiggle your fingers and toes, stretch and move, and when you're ready, open your eyes and begin to write.

Write down anything you just experienced from this past life, anything you want to remember, any insights that are coming to you.

Then, specifically address Archangel Raziel once more and ask him kindly to answer these questions:

Why did you bring me to this past life?

What do I need to learn from this?

What do I need to heal from this?

How can seeing this help me move forward in my current lifetime?

Is there anything else you'd like me to know?

Allow this to continue for as long as you'd like, and feel free to answer any questions that pop up in your own head.

Once finished, call upon Archangel Raziel and Archangel Raphael to help surround you in healing energy. Ask them to heal the past life you explored today, freeing you from its wounds if it was difficult or empowering you if it was joyful.

Afterward, send gratitude to Archangels Raziel and Raphael for being with you today and always.

GENERATIONAL INFLUENCES

Not only can our love life be affected by our previous incarnations, but our past in *this lifetime,* beyond our exes and mindset, can also have a major impact. Specifically, the way we were raised and who we were raised by.

Our parents, guardians, and family members have a major impact on how we see the world, what we believe about life, and especially what we believe about love. If growing up, the adults in our lives were negative or abusive, this will definitely contribute to the walls we put up and how we perceive love to be. Children with harsh guardians often subconsciously choose partners with similar traits as that is how they were taught to experience love.

Even if your guardians weren't obviously harmful, their words about you—remember when we went over identity in the Self-Love section?—can still affect how you perceive yourself and the type of love you think you deserve.

Situations where your parents or guardians were divorced, separated, or even stayed together in an unhappy marriage can shape your view of love and sometimes make you feel destined to repeat your parents'

or guardians' patterns. If you were raised by a single parent who just never found the right person, you may believe finding love also isn't possible for you. Maybe you grew up with the most loving, supportive LGBT parents and unfortunately witnessed the hate they received from narrow-minded people. This could have caused a fear within you that if you receive love, you'll also receive unfair judgement from others who will try to take it away. There are countless situations you could have experienced and witnessed as a child that now affect how you view love and relationships.

Healing that trauma around your parents' or guardians' relationships can be pivotal in opening your heart up to everlasting love. Generational healing is a vital part of healing your heart. Don't be afraid to dig deep into your past, into the words of your guardians and relatives. You may unbox some heavy things. However, think of them as forgotten old belongings in your basement. They need to go. You may not have thought about them for a while, but they're currently just sitting there, gathering dust, and taking up space. Cleaning them out and doing the work to let them go may be difficult and take a while, but your basement will be so much cleaner once you remove them, and then you have space to fill it with the things you love.

GENERATIONAL HEALING WITH ARCHANGEL RAPHAEL

This exercise may seem daunting, but remember you are deeply loved and supported. Archangel Raphael, the angel of healing, will gently guide you through this final step in releasing the past.

You can do this exercise as a meditation, seeing everything in your mind's eye, or you may like to use automatic writing and write down everything you are experiencing. Trust your intuition on this one and see which method feels right to you.

Scan the QR code to download and listen to the audio version of this meditation found at the back of this book.

Take a deep breath in and a deep breath out.

Take a deep breath in and a deep breath out.

Imagine angel wings sprouting from your back; beautiful, feathery wings unfurling behind you, growing stronger and wider.

Know that you, yourself, are an angel, sent here with the task of healing your lineage beyond just your own part in it.

You are pure strength itself. You are loved. You are divinely supported by all of your angels, especially Archangel Raphael.

You feel Archangel Raphael seated next to you; he lovingly grabs your hand, encouraging you that everything is alright.

As he grabs your hand, healing green energy extends into you. It fills your hand, your arm, your torso, your heart, your other arm, your other hand and flows across you in all directions. Some green light flows upward into your neck and head, while the rest of the green light flows downward into your sacral area, your legs, and feet.

The green light fills your entire body and then circles your entire aura.

The strongest glow stems from your heart chakra, where the green light sends extra healing energy to cleanse and clear every inch of your beautiful heart.

Feeling elevated on this plane of higher-level healing, you feel confident enough to handle what's before you; you feel confident enough to ask Archangel Raphael to show you what generational trauma you need to heal right now to help you move forward in love.

Allow the scene before you to shift as Raphael shows you either specific family members or an event that needs healing within your line. This event may have taken place during your lifetime, while you were in the womb, or it could have happened further back to your relatives before you were born.

Trust whatever is coming to you. Tap into what you are hearing, seeing, feeling, and just intuitively knowing.

Once you feel you've seen everything, ask Raphael, "What beliefs can I adopt or actions can I take to break this cycle and heal my generational line?"

Allow him to tell you.

Before moving forward, ask Raphael if there is anything else you need to see today.

Next, you are going to visualize your entire family tree standing tall and strong before you.

Imagine roots and branches that stretch out for miles and miles, each extending with the name of every single member of your family and every single one of your ancestors.

As you look at the tree, feel gratitude for all who came before you, understanding each one of them did the best they could with what they knew. Even if they weren't their best selves on Earth, once they reached the other side, they saw things from a higher perspective, and they, too, are here to assist you in this healing right now.

Feel Archangel Raphael standing next to you, and together, both of you, extend your hands wide, palms facing the tree.

Visualize green healing coming down from the divine and into the tree.

Healing rays of light come down from the divine and extend into you as you are now a channel for healing. Your hands feel warm, heating up, as the healing energy releases through your palms toward the tree. You send your own healing energy toward it as well.

Next to you, Archangel Raphael is also channeling healing energy, sending that green light into your tree.

The green light from you, Raphael, and the Universe flows through every single branch, through every leaf, every piece of bark, every root. It illuminates every piece of your family tree from top to bottom.

Divine healing extends throughout the past, into the present, and well into the future, healing from your very first relatives to walk the Earth, rippling through all of your ancestors. Feel the cleansing power of this healing energy as it moves through you. Then see it move to future descendants of your line, whether they are your own children who currently exist, will exist, or any offspring your siblings or cousins may have.

Once the entire tree feels healed, you lower your hands, as does Raphael, and you watch as the green light settles into the tree. The entire tree is glowing. You feel a strong sense of happiness and well-being, knowing that you just healed all generations across all timelines.

Archangel Raphael turns to you, smiles, and gives you a nod.

Know whenever you feel inclined, you may return to this place and add more healing to your lineage, but for now, it is completely refreshed and wholly healed.

Thank Archangel Raphael for all his help. Thank the Universe and thank your entire lineage.

Whenever you are ready, you may slowly start to return to your physical body, back to the room. Feel free to journal about any more feelings that come up for you.

HEALING THE SHADOW

Congratulations on doing all this healing. It's definitely not easy; shadow work (the process of diving into the darker parts of your story) is something most people tend to shy away from because it makes them uncomfortable. Facing the discomfort is the only way we can ever break free of it. That's exactly what you've done in this part.

Feel incredibly proud of yourself for being brave and facing these things. You are absolutely amazing.

As you move forward, know healing is an ongoing process, so be gentle with yourself. More things may come up, even things you thought you'd already healed, but know your angels, fairies, and mermaids are always here to support you. Healing happens in layers. So long as you are putting in the effort to do the healing work, one layer at a time, you'll get there.

I definitely recommend revisiting all of the exercises from this section any time you feel you need to.

Living in Love

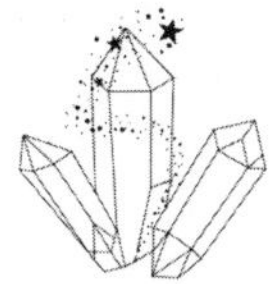

You've shifted your mindset; you've learned to see the beauty within yourself; you've released the past. Now, it's time to write your love story. It's time to manifest!

This is *your* life. You came here to be the author; you have the pen, the page is blank before you, and you decide what is written.

You've released all those limiting beliefs around love, and now it's time to energetically fill yourself with infinite possibilities, with divine magic, with romantic happily ever afters.

DAILY VISUALIZING

I love to start my morning with positive intentions. Remember, your identity and your embodiment are everything. This is such a simple exercise and something that takes no time at all but will make a big difference. Whether you have to rush to work or have kids to take care of, you can squeeze this in.

When you first open your eyes, instead of instantly worrying about all the things you have to do or maybe even dreading your day ahead, give yourself a moment of peace. Even if you only have two minutes before you have to physically get out of bed, fill those moments with good vibes.

Call upon Archangel Chamuel to help you find pleasant things throughout your day, and ask Archangel Jophiel to help you see the beauty in your life. Call upon the fairies to believe in magic and have fun, and call upon the mermaids to tune into your intuition.

For a moment or two before you get up, think about things you're grateful for.

Set intentions: *Today is going to be a great day. Everything is going to work in my favor. I radiate good luck and good energy.*

And that's all!

If you are fortunate to have more time to lay in bed, you have more time to think about all the beautiful things you want to manifest in love and play into the idea that they are already yours.

If you have to get up straight away, as you're getting ready for your day, keep thinking about all the things you're grateful for and focusing on the idea that today can be a great one.

Set intentions for love.

While the following example may be a money-manifesting one rather than one for love, I know applying the energy and intention behind it will work exactly the same.

One summer, when working in a summer camp, I woke up every single morning, thanked my angels, fairies, and mermaids, and stated it was going to be a great day. I also set the intention to call in an extra seven hundred and fifty dollars. I was open to it coming in any way, and I believed, without a doubt, that it was mine.

On the last day of the summer camp, I received generous tips from parents, equaling $650. Even though it wasn't the full amount I set my intentions for, I was still so incredibly grateful to the Universe for receiving this money. Then, right before I left for the day, my camp director called me into his office and gave me an extra $100 for gas money because he was so grateful that I drove some of the other counselors to camp all summer long. That brought my total to $750, just as I had set my intention for every single day!

Why not do the same for love? Why not wake up every day feeling thankful that you already have your partner? Or with the intention that you are meeting the love of your life today? Feel it in your heart, know it, and believe it! Love may show up when you least expect it in a way you never imagined.

SET THE SCENE FOR LOVE

Get creative as you embody the version of you who already has love. The biggest keys to manifesting are embodiment and surrendering to the Universe's plan.

Let go of any timelines, the when, the where, and the how, and act like love is already yours. Know without a doubt and pretend it's your reality.

If you're eating dinner alone, set another spot at the table for your true love. When you're driving, don't put your purse or any other items in your passenger seat; keep it clear as if the love of your life needs a space to sit. Pack a romantic picnic to bring to the park, sit there, eat, and pretend the love of your life is on their way to meet you. Create space for them to exist in your life.

Romanticize your life. Start to turn *everything* into an enchanting romance. Buy yourself flowers, and go on adventures. Even if you're sitting at home, wear your dreamiest attire. Pretend your tea is a love potion, drink out of fancy glasses, light a candle with every meal, play high-vibe music as you get ready, and go watch the sunsets.

Make a digital vision board with romantic vibes and set it as your phone background. As you're driving, pretend you're en route to the airport to go to Paris or Bora Bora or somewhere dreamy and magical. When you go out to run errands, pretend you're on a mystical quest. Write journal entries with multi-colored glitter pens. Sit outside and paint. Make wishes on stars. Wear whimsical charm bracelets. Write love letters to the Universe. Decorate your space with crystals and fairy lights. Walk through a flower garden and look for butterflies. Sit and watch the ocean. Wear a crown, wear fairy wings, wear sequins and sparkles. Talk to plants and animals. Visit a magnificent library or a castle.

And, of course, take romantic, intention-fueled baths.

LOVE INTENTION BATH WITH THE MERMAIDS

As water elementals, it makes sense that the most prominent way to connect with the mermaids' energy is through water. With this exercise, you don't need to live anywhere near the ocean or any body of water, as you can do this from the comfort of your own home.

For this exercise, you are going to make the most magical mermaid bath of your dreams! (If you don't have a bath, this exercise can easily be adapted for an amazing everything shower. Imagine it's a waterfall!)

Fill your tub with water and add bath salts to simulate the saltiness of the ocean. Salt water also helps clear out all of your chakras, so know this bath will not only help you manifest, but it will also energetically cleanse you.

Surround your bathroom with seashells, aquamarine crystals, and other sea-themed items, like pearl necklaces, anchors, golden treasure, or mermaid statues. Play ambient music of the ocean, waves curling into the shore, seagulls calling. You can even add a fan to simulate that gentle ocean breeze.

Safely light blue or pink candles (or both!), as pink helps us call in love, and blue helps us communicate what we want. Feel the intention of love as you light your candle; as you watch the wick ignite, feel the flames of romance spark into your heart.

When the vibe feels right, step into your bath. If you have long hair, let it down to feel more of that mystical mermaid energy.

As you're in the bath, thank the mermaids for their support, wisdom, and guidance, and spend all your time there visualizing the romance of your dreams. Don't focus your energy on love with a specific person; instead, leave it open and set intentions for whoever is for your highest good. Feel all the emotions of divine love. Imagine all the smiles, the butterflies, the pure joy as if you were already with the partner of your dreams. See yourself going on dates, getting married (if you so wish), holding hands, and sharing kisses. Pretend it's all happening now.

Ask the mermaids to help you fully surrender, to let go of stressing about when, where, or how (even as you move beyond this bath!). Set aside any worries or doubts and fully give in to the idea: *It's happening now! This is actually my life!* By doing so, you're energetically sending all those vibes out into the Universe, and it's only a matter of time before true love manifests.

When you're finished, thank the mermaids for helping you tap into your emotions, thank them for inspiring romance, and, as always, send them either a gift in your mind's eye or the next time you visit the ocean.

MAKE A FAIRY WAND

Another great way to romanticize your life and manifest your true love is to make your own fairy wand. This is one of my favorite exercises; I love recommending it to clients who adore the fantasy vibe.

When you make your own wand, it helps you channel your natural manifesting power. It's empowering to think about exactly what you want, feel it in your heart, and then wave your wand, imagining yourself casting the spell to bring it to you. Always add, "… or whatever is for my highest good!" at the end of any statement you make when waving your wand. Remember, sometimes, what we want may be delayed intentionally because it's not meant for us, but something *better* is! Be crystal clear with your intentions, but also leave room for magic. Leave room for the Universe, fairies, mermaids, and angels to bring you to your destiny.

With that, it's time to make your fairy wand.

A great way to start is to collect a sturdy stick or branch that has naturally fallen (it's disrespectful to rip it from a tree). Find one you feel drawn to, and, of course, ask the forest, the surrounding nature area, or the nearest tree if you have permission to use it. Tune into your intuition and wait until you feel a "yes". If you feel the "yes", then proceed. If you feel a "no", then keep searching.

Once you have your branch, adorn it with whatever you'd like. You can wrap it with some pretty ribbons and dried flowers or use gold wire to wrap some crystals around. As this wand will help you manifest love, I'd recommend including mini rose quartz chips or rose quartz in the shape of a tiny heart!

You may paint words like *magic*, *love* or *abundance* on it, or you can even carve Elder Futhark runes into it.

Runes are ancient, powerful symbols. Each one holds a specific vibration. They were used by Nordic and Germanic people to call for more protection, wealth, good luck, etc. If you intend to use these, I'd encourage you to do some additional research and use them with the highest respect.

If the runes feel aligned with you, I recommend using three of my favorites. Wunjo for victory, joy, and a happily ever after; Sowelio which represents the sun, good vibes, and your time to shine; and Gifu for blessings, gifts, and unexpected positive surprises. I actually wore two necklaces adorned with the symbols of Wunjo and Sowelio on my wedding day to bring in sunshine, joy, and happily-ever-after energy.

Use any other adornments that feel aligned and customize your wand to your soul.

When you're done, hold your wand to your heart and infuse it with your energy. Set your intentions into it, pour love and gratitude into it, and know your wand is an extension of your power.

Every time you wish to manifest love and romance, state what you want, wave your wand, and know you are materializing it into existence.

VISUALIZATION TO ROMANTICIZE YOUR LIFE

Along with taking a mermaid bath and crafting a fairy wand, I recommend making a list of all the ways you can romanticize your life. For more ideas, here is a simple meditation to connect to either the fairies or the mermaids (your choice!) and ask them for advice on how you can romanticize your life. They'll also show you what your life would look like if you dedicated yourself to romanticizing the everyday.

I recommend doing this visualization often, perhaps trying it first with the fairies, then again with the mermaids, as the more you visualize and feel the more you manifest.

Scan the QR code to download and listen to the audio version of this meditation found at the back of this book.

Take a deep breath in and a deep breath out.

Take a deep breath in and a deep breath out

Imagine sparkling golden energy surrounding you, encompassing you, and filling every inch of your aura.

Start to see a stunning scene unfold before you, the most romantic setting you can imagine. Maybe it's an abundant rose garden; a beach at sunset; a candlelit library; or an ornate castle. Whatever it is, trust what you see.

Feel your heart chakra radiating with love.

Your heart is fully opened, expanded, and ready to tap into your most romantic life.

Tune into the beautiful, mystical energy of the fairies or the mermaids, whomever you feel intuitively guided to call upon today. Or ask for whoever wants to be with you right now.

Call upon your fairies or mermaids and state you are only available to interact with beings of the highest level of light and love, with the purest intention for all.

In your mind's eye, offer a gift to your fairies or mermaids with a gift as a token of appreciation and invite them to be with you.

Feel their sparkling presence emerge, exchange pleasantries, and ask them: What are some ways I can be more like you and romanticize my life?

Allow them to show you.

Once you're done, ask them: Please show me, how my life would look if I dedicated myself to romanticizing my life.

Allow them to show you, and as you see the scenes unfold before, truly tune into how it would feel to actually be experiencing this.

Feel into the love, feel into the magic, and of course, feel into the romance.

When you're done, thank your fairies or mermaids for all their guidance today.

Know that by feeling and seeing all of this, you have sent that romantic energy out into the universe and it is, without a doubt, going to come back to you and manifest into your life.

Continue to embody these feelings moving forward, take the fairies' and mermaids' advice on romanticizing your life, and know that what you just saw will soon be your reality.

Take one more deep breath in and a deep breath out…and, when you're ready, slowly return to the room, knowing you are now set to live your best, most romanticized life!

Feel free to journal about anything you experienced.

MAKE A VIRTUAL VISION BOARD

You look at your phone (and most likely computer) every single day—so why not allow yourself to manifest while you do so?

A classic manifestation tool that most traditional teachers often suggest creating is a vision board—a collage filled with the imagery of all the things you desire. When you look at your board, you can train your brain to believe you already have everything pictured. This is a great tool; however, I think it's even better when it's done virtually and placed as your phone's lock screen or computer background.

Imagine every time you pick up your phone or open your laptop, instead of mindlessly wondering about your notifications, you intentionally see scenes that light your soul up with all the romance you want to experience. You give your brain an excuse to take a moment to feel it as if it's already yours!

Make a digital collage and fill it with pictures that evoke all the feelings you want to manifest in love. Include a silhouette of a couple holding hands on a sunset beach, maybe add a wedding ring if you wish to get married, flowers, vacation spots, a home you'd like to share, and a pet you'd like to have together. Whatever lights your soul up, add it to your collage.

I also like to add text to my virtual vision boards, including words I want to experience like *fun*, *adventure,* and *romance*. You can also add empowering romance affirmations, ones that support the love story you'd like to write, and every time you look at your phone, you can recite them.

My friend Cecilia loves to set affirmation alarms. At scheduled times, like 1:11 p.m., 2:22 p.m., 3:33 p.m., 4:44 p.m., and 5:55 p.m., she has set alarms on her phone to remind her to read and recite empowering affirmations. These provide her with excuses every hour to feel the vibration of the energy she wants to call in and manifest.

Love Affirmations for your Phone

I am worthy of living the most
magical true love story.

I am loved. I am in love. I am love.

I am so happy and grateful to have
the most amazing partner.

I am so happy and grateful to be joyously in a
healthy relationship with the love of my life.

I am divinely loved and supported.

I am a magnet for love and romance.

I am lucky in love!

Tune into your intuition to create the best affirmations for you. Once you've created a virtual vision board that feels aligned, set it as your phone and computer background. Every time you unlock your device, you'll feel a fresh surge of joy upon seeing everything that makes you smile. This will naturally help you tune into the energy of everything you want to manifest.

Your subconscious brain doesn't know the difference between a picture and an experience, so if it's constantly *seeing* something, it will align itself with that frequency. It's all about normalizing love and romance in your life. Once your subconscious brain has accepted love and romance as your truth, it makes it easier for it to become your reality.

LOVE IS EVERYWHERE

So much of manifesting is about experiencing the feelings first. If we want to manifest joy and happiness, we need to feel joy and happiness *now*. If we want to manifest abundance, we need to find ways to feel abundant *now*. Therefore, if we want love and romance, we need to find ways to feel loved now. The feelings create the experience, not the other way around.

Along with focusing your mindset and aligning your words and thoughts, make sure you feel loved right now by recognizing all the ways love currently exists in your life.

Open your eyes and notice how much certain friends adore you and you, them. See how certain family members care for you and you, them. Notice the way your pet loves you and you, them. You know what it's like to love unconditionally thanks to your pets, your best friends, and your family. Recognizing that you are *already* loved and already have love abundantly present in your life helps elevate you to the frequency of someone who already has love.

As you've learned, the Universe matches the frequency you radiate on. If you're on a frequency of actively appreciating how much love exists in your life, the Universe is going to find *more* ways to bring it to you.

Not only do the people and pets in our lives elevate us to that frequency of love, but so do the things we're passionate about. Just as we did in an earlier exercise with Archangel Jophiel, don't forget to continually take notice of the things that fill your heart with love. Maybe it's a certain book series you're obsessed with. Maybe it's a film. Maybe it's a theme park. Maybe it's fresh fruit smoothies. Maybe it's springtime. Maybe it's ice skating. Maybe it's tiny little ladybugs or purses with bows on them. Maybe it's going to art museums or tea parties.

I'm sure that throughout your life, you've encountered uncountable things that you love, things that you're happy to experience, and that make you feel glad to be human. Regularly indulging more in your favorite things helps boost that frequency of love. If cheering on your favorite sports team makes your heart happy—go to games as often as you can. If baking cupcakes fills you up with joy—do more of that. Whether it's eating pizza, going to the movies, or dressing head to toe in lavender-colored clothes, whatever you love, integrate more and more of it into your everyday life. Not only will this make you smile, but it also raises your energetic vibration, surrounding you in that bubble of love. Feeling love will always be one of the best ways to manifest even more of it in your life.

LISTEN TO YOUR FEELINGS

While you're trying to create the feelings now, make sure you're also simultaneously listening to your natural feelings. Your emotions are one of your greatest gifts, as they are your intuitive guidance system. This is a lesson the mermaids continually try to teach us.

Your emotions are clueing you into what is aligned with your soul and what is out of alignment with your soul. It seems a little obvious, but it's something we so often overlook. If something or someone continually feels bad or wrong, that's your soul telling you that person or thing is out of alignment with you.

When my husband and I were still just co-workers, I'd experience overwhelming happiness whenever he'd come into the office. I was inexplicably excited to see him.

I realize now that my emotions were telling me he *was* aligned with my soul.

Similarly, I can recall previous romantic encounters when my date would just feel *off*. Even if the person was seemingly fine, I felt strangely anxious or sad. In those cases, my emotions and my intuition were trying to tell me those people were out of alignment.

I don't mean feeling off on a one-time basis. That shouldn't be cause for concern. We all have days where we feel sad, overwhelmed, or mad. That's normal. Life is cyclical, and we're going to have ups and downs. As humans, we are going to feel the full spectrum of the emotional scale—and we should fully allow ourselves to. What I mean is if you are *consistently* feeling off every single day, that's when you should recognize that emotions are trying to warn you that something happening is out of alignment and needs to be adjusted. This is when it's great to journal about your feelings to make sense of what they are trying to tell you. Call upon the mermaids to assist as you write out everything you are feeling about… well, everything!

Similar to the Feelings Rant we did at the beginning of the book, regularly giving yourself time and space to write all your feelings out will help you gain clarity about what's currently going on and what needs to change. I recommend making a weekly journaling date with yourself and the mermaids to check in with what your emotions are clueing you into.

All you have to do is call upon the mermaids' energy, thank them, and then turn to your journal and ask them to help you be honest with yourself. Ask the mermaids to open your third eye and tune into your intuition so you can clearly understand what your emotions are trying to tell you. This prompt will help you get started:

I feel [write how you feel], *so that means [*the situation/ person/etc] *is currently* [*in/ out*] *of alignment with my highest self. The best way for me to move forward would be to* [write what intuitive guidance comes to you / whatever you feel the mermaids telling you].

Trust whatever pops into your head, trust your instincts.

Once you've checked in with your emotions and gained a better understanding of what they are trying to tell you, it's a perfect time to manifest.

MERMAID MESSAGE IN A BOTTLE

Scan the QR code to download and listen to the audio version of this meditation found at the back of this book.

Take a deep breath in and a deep breath out.

Take a deep breath in and a deep breath out.

Picture standing on a beautiful ocean shore as turquoise waves gently sweep in and out, tickling your toes. Warm honey-colored sand radiates beneath your feet. You inhale the light scent of salt air and coconuts as an ocean breeze flitters through your hair. The sky is ablaze with a stunning orange sunset adorned with clouds of the most vibrant pink, yellow, and white.

In the distance, floating closer and closer to you, a sparkle of something catches your eye.

You wait as the tides bring it in closer and closer. Eventually, you see it's a glass bottle with a message inside it, and someone seems to be carrying it straight to you as if delivering it.

You wade a few steps into the water to meet a mermaid smiling at you. They hand you the bottle, telling you it's a message from your true love.

You open it as butterflies flutter in your stomach and excitement floods through your veins. You read every detail with the biggest grin on your face. You can feel the love radiating from the message as you read the words your true love has written, sharing how much they can't wait to meet you and have the most magical romance.

You look to the mermaid messenger. They smile at you, present you with paper and pen, and tell you to write your response.

Now, it's time to write.

Get yourself a pen, a piece of paper, and a glass bottle.

Write the most romantic letter to your true love, saying everything you wish to say to them. Tell them how much you can't wait to meet them, describe all the hopes and dreams you have for the two of you, let them know how much they already mean to you, and detail the kind of romance you know you'll have.

Pour out the contents of your heart, and when you're done, seal the message with love and put it in the bottle. Put a golden trinket or charm next to your bottle (maybe some seashells as well) as a token of your appreciation for the mermaid messenger.

Visualize yourself back on that mystical beach, and imagine handing the bottle to your mermaid messenger. See them smiling at you, and imagine giving them the trinket as appreciation for their help.

You thank them and watch as they nod, take your message, and swim off into the sea, delivering this message and all the love within to your true love.

Keep your bottle somewhere safe, maybe on an altar or surrounded by crystals. Every time you look at it, think of your true love and send them well wishes and loving energy. Believe you are in correspondence with each other and feel excited that every single day you become a day closer to meeting.

You can continue writing more love letters as often as you'd like, adding each one to your bottle, and offering a gift of thanks to your mermaid messenger each time.

COMMIT TO LOVE

Continually find ways to romanticize your life. Pretend you're the main character in a fantasy romance novel and be swept up in the idea that you already have the love of your life. If you can constantly convince yourself, your energy will radiate with love and the Universe will match that frequency. The more consistently you believe, the more powerful and activated the energetic path between you and your love becomes. The Universe favors the path of least resistance so it's only a matter of time before love rushes into your life in the earthly realm.

Keep believing, even *while* you're working through all your mindset shifts and releasing the past exercises. Remember, it's okay to be a work in progress; as humans, we're all works in progress. Know it's still possible to manifest even while you're working through the things you need to work through. The only thing that will ever stop you from manifesting is if you stop believing or give up. So long as you believe in yourself, the Universe, your fairies, angels, and mermaids, and believe in magic, *of course,* true love is going to come to you eventually. True love is going to come to you in divine timing.

Never give up hope. You got this.

LOVE IS IN THE AIR - FAIRY MANIFESTATION

Remember as a child when you'd find the fluffy white dandelions and make a wish by blowing their seeds? That's exactly what we're going to do now.

Find a dandelion. Ask for its permission to pick it; wait until you receive a clear "yes," and if you do, send it lots of love and gratitude whilst plucking it. Then, you're going to call upon a specific type of fairy, the sylphs.

Sylphs exist in the wind and help purify the skies by removing pollution and toxins. They also bring about the vibe of *love being in the* air. They help sweep us off our feet with romance and carry our wishes of love aloft.

Hold your dandelion to your heart and make your most romantic wish. Feel it, dream it, and believe it.

Then, as you blow the dandelion, ask the beautiful sylphs to carry your wish skywards; watch as the dandelion seeds are swept up in the wind, just as you'll be swept up in romance!

Thank the sylphs tremendously for their efforts. Leave them a gift as a token of your appreciation, such as a treat, a treasure, or even a gift reminiscent of the sky (like sky-themed crystals like celestite).

WRITING YOUR LOVE STORY

Get out a journal and start with the classic words: "Once upon a time."

Call upon the fairies, mermaids, and angels to support you as you let your wildest dreams bloom to life on the page.

Write *your* story, your fairy tale, happily ever after without limitations.

Imagine the most romantic love story you can think of. What would make you swoon if you read it in a romance novel? Make those things part of your story!

Set yourself as the main character, create the dreamiest love interest for yourself, and fuel your heart with bliss as you fill the blank pages with everything you could ever hope for *and more*. Write it all as if it is a fairy tale someone else is reading one day, a love story that gives them hope and inspiration.

Of course, don't forget to end with "And they lived happily ever after."

Write as if it has all already happened. Get creative and make sure you are feeling emotionally connected as you're writing. Let your imagination take you wherever your heart wants to go and know that as you're writing, you're manifesting!

Your Happily Ever After

You are a beautiful soul. Your journey has not always been easy, but your perseverance is admirable. The fact that you've made it to the end of this book shows that you are willing to put in the effort. You acknowledged you needed to make a change, and you dedicated yourself to learning and trying something new—and with that mindset, anything is possible for you!

You deserve the most incredible true love story. You deserve fireworks and romance; you deserve heart-glowing happiness, mind-blowing intimacy, and a touch that feels electric. You deserve to feel elated, smile so hard your face hurts, feel safe and secure, and experience loyalty and respect. You deserve giggles and silliness. You deserve to be swept away on an adventure and feel like you're the protagonist of a fairy tale. You deserve kindness and support; you deserve your best friend.

I know life will bring you the most amazing partner to fall deeper and deeper in love with every day, and I also hope you fall deeper in love with yourself. Remember, while the right partner can add value to your life, true happiness originates from within you!

It's all coming together for you. You are capable of creating magic because you truly are a divinely, innately, immensely enchanting soul supported by a host of incredible beings. I hope you absolutely adored getting to know the angels, fairies, and mermaids as you worked with them in all these rituals. You don't have to find an excuse to talk to them; feel free to connect with them on a regular basis, any time you wish. They are more than happy to help you add that extra boost of magic into your life.

Once you've manifested your true love, you can continue to work with your angels, fairies, and mermaids to help that love blossom and bloom every single day. Don't be afraid once your love has arrived. You are more than capable of maintaining love. You have nothing to fear. Ask your angels, mermaids, and fairies to remind you that you are worthy of this love. Just because it seems "too good to be true" doesn't mean it's going to all go away. If it's "too good to be true," trust that it can *just be true*, and accept it as a beautiful blessing from the Universe.

Once you have your love, it's up to both you and your partner to continually put in the effort to maintain that true love. Get into a habit of showing each other consistent gratitude and adoration. Allow yourself to receive compliments and be showered with love as you give the same to them.

Create romance with your partner. Romanticize your life every single day, and romanticize your life *together*! Have fun; laugh; go on dates. Make life magical. Grow together. Hear each other out. Talk it out. Listen. Express yourself. Work together to understand one another and allow each other space to bloom. Support one another. Help each other. Lift each other up. Hype each other up. You're a team, an iconic duo, and you will always have each other's backs. Keep your heart open to this love and know it is the best. Your relationship will evolve and grow over time, but the love will stay. True love will always remain because you manifested it to be so!

Remember, you don't just receive a magical love story—you create it!

See the beauty in your journey *now* and know absolutely everything is unfolding for you. Celebrate yourself. Celebrate your life and celebrate your love. This is just the start, and all your wishes in love are on their way to becoming your reality.

May your life forever be filled with love and happiness.

May you truly live your magical ever after.

Scan the QR code to download and listen to the audio versions of the meditations found throughout this magical book

ABOUT ERICA ROSE

Erica Rose is an Author, Intuitive, and Spiritual Teacher from Long Island, New York, devoted to helping others rediscover their magic and manifest lives filled with love, joy, and purpose. Her spiritual journey began at sixteen, when a clairvoyant grandmother revealed that intuition is not just a gift for the few, but a power we all hold. Since then, Erica has spent over a decade guiding others in connecting with angels, mermaids, faeries, and their own soul's wisdom.

Specializing in manifestation, past life healing, and intuition development, Erica empowers her clients and readers to become the authors of their own fairy tales. Her teachings blend grounded mindset practices with enchanted spiritual tools, inviting people to awaken their inner magic and co-create with the divine.

Her greatest manifestation?
A real-life love story with her husband, Justin—proof that magic and miracles are more than possible when you're aligned with your heart.